Leading Innovation

Creating Workplaces Where People Excel So Organizations Thrive

Brian McDermott and Gerry Sexton

Also available from Nova Vista Publishing:

Win-Win Selling
Vendre gagnant-gagnant (French edition of Win-Win Selling)
Versatile Selling
S'adapter à mieux vendre (French edition of Versatile Selling)
Socal Styles Handbook
I Just Love my Job!

How to order: single copies may be ordered online at www.novavistapub.com.
In North America, you may phone 503-590-8898. Elsewhere, dial +32-14-21-11-21.

ISBN 90-77256-05-9

D/2004/9797/2

Printed and bound in Canada

20 19 18 17 16 15 14 13 12 11 10 9 8 7 6 5 4 3 2

Editorial development: Andrew Karre
Cover design: Astrid de Deyne
Text design: Layout Sticker

Contents

SECTION 3: OBSTACLES – WHAT'S IN THE WAY OF INNOVATION?

Foreword

For almost twenty-five years I was a fulltime educator – largely at the Harvard Business School. I taught in the areas of Organizational Behavior and Change, Human Resource Management, Strategy, and Service Management. Despite the learning opportunities this experience provided, I was profoundly underdeveloped in the critically important area of leading innovation when I moved into my role as Vice Chairman and Chief Operating Officer at Limited Brands, operator of more than 3,800 stores and six retail brands, including Victoria's Secret, Bath & Body Works, Express, and The Limited. I know I was not alone in this shortcoming, because during my years in academia I had the opportunity to participate in field research in hundreds of organizations around the world and to work as a consultant with some of the most progressive organizations and leaders of our time.

In part, this all-too-common problem stems from underestimating or not contemplating well enough the overwhelming environmental shifts and competitive pressures that face our particular businesses or industries, which in my case is specialty retail. To a greater extent, this missed opportunity to grow and excel represents a profound lack of recognition of the powerful forces of homeostasis – the tendency of most complex systems to reach a state of equilibrium. The sense of balance that comes from operating in a stable environment is seductive. It masquerades as comfort. But it also leads to inertia – a powerful and limiting force.

Even the most talented and well-intended individuals, if they are enveloped by the contentment of the status quo, don't generally recognize their condition – or the ensuing risks that stagnation presents to their businesses. Management scholars and consultants label the phenomenon "resistance to change," and prescribe countless varieties of "silver bullet solutions" to overcome it. But the true problem is unrecognizable and virtually indescribable – unless you have the language and insights to convey passion and unique perspectives about leading innovation effectively.

There is no question that the pace of innovation in modern organizations must increase. Unfortunately, there is ample empirical evidence that the strategies most often used to allocate resources to support innovation generally fall short. Investing in research and development is essential, for example, but that alone it is not enough. To meet the critical challenges of innovation, today's leaders must improve the *structures and processes of human interaction*. This book offers a significant, practical contribution to the leader's arsenal of ideas, tools, and tactics for doing just that, in all facets of organizational life.

Leading Innovation is a gem of a text that takes a strikingly different position about *how* to make innovation happen. Instead of focusing on overcoming resistance, Brian McDermott's and Gerry Sexton's LOOP Leadership approach builds upon a fundamental premise: the best route to creativity and innovation is through an inclusive model of leadership that brings out the best that each individual in an organization has to offer. They follow up with a wealth of intervention tools, techniques, and approaches that effectively tie to and support their model.

The underlying premise of *Leading Innovation* is deceptively simple – get people creatively, strategically, and energetically involved – but in reality, so also is some of the actual work of innovation. I encourage you to test out many of the intervention ideas in this book. I have little doubt you will see significant results as you help the people you work with take the lead on generating and implementing ideas for change and improvement. After all, that's the whole point of leadership!

Leading Innovation is destined to become an important contribution to the archives on positive organizational leadership practices. The insights and techniques you will find in this book can advance your knowledge and skill in this most critical area of leadership. Use them well.

Leonard A. Schlesinger

Vice Chairman and Chief Operating Officer, Limited Brands

Former George F. Baker Jr. Professor of Business Administration, Harvard Business School

Columbus, Ohio, USA

August, 2004

OPENING THE LOOP ON INNOVATION

Chapter 1

The Art of Innovative Leadership

"No man can reveal to you aught but that which already lies half asleep in the dawning of your knowledge. The teacher who walks in the shadow of the temple, among his followers, gives not of his wisdom but rather of his faith and his lovingness. If he is indeed wise he does not bid you enter the house of his wisdom, but rather leads you to the threshold of your own mind."

—KAHLIL GIBRAN

Leadership isn't rocket science. Our experience says that great leadership is far more complex than that – especially when it comes to leading innovation.

If you have people reporting to you, you know that life in the workplace can get complicated in a hurry. Sure, delivering cosmonauts to the International Space Station or landing a rover on Mars are complex challenges laden with millions of logistical variables. But imagine bringing together 100 managers from around the world who have been working independently and telling them they are being reorganized into one worldwide virtual team – and that *everything* about the way they have been working is about to change. This was the leadership challenge for a client of ours who wished she *only* had to land a probe on a passing comet.

Science and math at least provide verifiable theorems and procedures about how to rendezvous with moving objects in space. Leading people, however, is much more of an art than a science, and it's far too unpredictable to be accurately calculated by any algorithms we know about.

Perhaps the most limiting myth perpetuated in the world of business is that every organization encourages its people to be creative and innovative. People are, always have been, and always will be any organization's most valuable asset. There's probably not a business leader on the planet who hasn't said those very words. Your boss has probably said them to you. You've probably shared the same message in your own way with the people you lead. And we all mean what we say. The reality, however, is that many organizations systematically repress, neglect, or overlook – often unwittingly – the ideas, talents, and energy people innately long to contribute to their work.

Even with the best of intentions, actions often fall short of words. The result: Individuals exist, but they don't excel. Organizations survive, but they don't thrive.

Why?

Everybody agrees innovation is critically important. We talk about it – and people write about it – all the time. But the bulk of what you'll find in the media focuses on the need for it – often very passionately, with wisdom and commitment. However, what we want to address in *Leading Innovation* is specifically *how* you, as a leader, can make innovation part of your team's or organization's soul.

When you ask the people you lead to be innovative, you're asking them to do things differently, to change, to improve, to let go of the old ways of doing business – even if those old ways have led to ongoing success. You are inviting uncertainty, the risk of failure, and a degree of chaos into an otherwise relatively controlled environment. It's no wonder that even if we buy in on the concept, we send mixed messages and struggle with the *how*.

For some of the people you lead, your call for innovation will be the best possible news they could hear. They thrive on challenge and change, and they love the idea of unleashing their imaginations. They may be dying to stretch themselves. For others, this is news from their worst nightmares. They're competent, comfortable, and content to do what they've always done. They've got their jobs more or less under control, and they will invest plenty of energy to keep things that way. Your challenge is to harness all of the human potential that lies on the continuum between these two reactions and focus it toward your ultimate responsibility as a leader – the performance outcomes of your team.

That can be tough duty.

A critical, simple concept

The good news is that our solution for this complex challenge comes in the shape of a relatively simple concept: *Your success in leading innovation depends on your willingness and ability to unshackle the energy, ideas and talents that your people can – and want to – pour into their work with you.*

Marcus Buckingham, a researcher and a global-practice leader at the Gallup Organization in Chicago, considered this challenge in the groundbreaking work that led him to co-author *First Break All the Rules: What the World's Greatest Managers Do Differently.* One of those rules, based on studies with 100,000 managers in 400 different companies, is: "Stop trying to change people. Start trying to help them become more of who they already are."

That advice, he warns, is contradictory to the natural impulse many leaders feel about the need to control every aspect of their operations. He told *Fast Company* magazine that "CEOs hate variance. It's the enemy." Buckingham argues that CEOs stamp out all variance – both good and bad – because it makes their jobs less complex and more predictable.

"There is, however, one resource inside all companies that will hinder any attempt to eliminate variance: each individual's personality." Buckingham says that there's no way to eliminate the variations in human personality and get a perfectly uniform workforce – and he's right, of course. But he's also right when he says that's exactly what most managers try to do: they try to standardize human behavior.

"Not only is that approach psychologically daft, it's hugely inefficient," he says. "It's fighting human nature, and anyone who fights human nature will lose."

The Gallup research shows that leaders who excel at getting great performance from the people they lead don't try to re-wire people or try to put in what was left out. Instead, they try to draw out the gifts and energy that are already there, just waiting to be tapped.

"When it comes to getting the best performance out of people, the most efficient route is to revel in their strengths, not to focus on their weaknesses," concludes Buckingham.

In *Leading Innovation,* we offer an uncomplicated solution for a very complicated problem. Not surprisingly, it comes with the caveat that "simple to grasp" does not mean "easy to implement."

Open the gates for creativity

Letting go can be a scary proposition. That's especially true for leaders who believe they must be in control of absolutely everything that happens in their areas. But enlightened leaders know they must define and constantly communicate the endgame – the desired outcome – *and* free people to figure out how to get there. They free people to ask questions, challenge the status quo, take risks, try things that have never been tried before, and fail. In doing so, they create an environment where people excel, not merely exist.

There are exceptions, we are certain, but we don't know many people who go to work every day saying, "I'm going in there today to see how many things I can screw up."

For decades, 3M has been recognized as one of the most innovative companies in the world. Each year, the Minnesota-based company introduces hundreds of new products, secures hundreds of new patents, and brings in tens of millions of dollars in revenue from new products and services. That success stems in large part from a foundation laid by William M. McKnight, whose tenure at the company included serving as president and then CEO from 1929 to 1966. That's a remarkably long career by any measure.

In 1948, McKnight urged managers to delegate responsibility, and even to tolerate mistakes, to stimulate good people to take initiative in their work. He conceded in an internal policy statement that,

> Mistakes will be made. But if a person is essentially right, the mistakes he or she makes are not as serious, in the long run, as the mistakes management will make if it's dictatorial ....
>
> Management that is destructively critical when mistakes are made kills initiative, and it's essential that we have many people with initiative if we are to continue to grow.

Even in organizations trying desperately to emulate this philosophy, it can be difficult for individual leaders to create and sustain the kind of a workplace that consistently nurtures innovation. One of the first times we tested this theory, we asked sixty managers in a $500-million division of a high-tech client company to conduct a walk-around survey as part of a leadership development process we created. We sent them out into their headquarters offices to get an instant read on some work-climate issues related to leading innovation.

The first question we had them ask employees was, "Do you believe the average employee in this company has ideas that could help make us more successful?" The second question was, "Do you believe the average employee is regularly asked to contribute ideas to make this company more successful?"

The managers plotted their responses one at a time on a bar chart at the front of the room as they returned to our meeting space. It didn't take long for them to recognize the gates for creativity in their organization needed a big squirt of oil on the hinges. More than 95 percent of those surveyed said they believed the average employee had ideas to help make the company more successful, but more than 95 percent also said they were not regularly asked to contribute those ideas. This disconnect, perceived or real, kills the very initiative McKnight believed was vital to cultivate. A 3M that didn't ask for ideas would be a 3M that probably would have killed the now-legendary Post-it Note.

Relationships and involvement are critical ingredients

Two premises underlie the experience and advice we have to share with you about leading innovation:

1. Your **relationship** with the people you lead is one of the most critical factors in creating a workplace where people excel.

Nothing is more important in determining how long employees stay and how productive they are than the relationship they have with you, their direct supervisor. People do not leave companies – they leave managers.

2. One of the most effective ways to ensure productive relationships is to **engage and involve the people you lead in important ways** in your work together.

In nearly every employee satisfaction survey we have ever seen, challenging and meaningful work are consistently critical factors in ensuring people feel positive about the work they do. Challenge and meaning become clearer and stronger the more you involve people in the decisions that influence their individual work and the objectives of the organization.

It is that simple – and that complicated.

The LOOP Leadership Model

In line with those two underlying premises, we've created one model to organize the advice, tools, examples, lessons, and stories we offer to help you create workplaces where people will excel and help make your organization thrive. We call it LOOP Leadership.

"LOOP" is an acronym for four challenges leaders must address in order to lead innovation:

Linkage

Obstacles

Opportunities

Plans

It's no accident that the acronym we created to organize our thinking and teaching about leading innovation is built on a familiar old maxim: People want to be kept *in the loop* on things. In matters that are important to us, we all want to be informed about what's happening and hope we can be appropriately involved in decisions that will influence our lives. It is also helpful to think of the LOOP Model as a ring connecting the four steps and indicating the cyclical and continuous nature of the work required to lead innovation. Although the model is not linear, it is important, as you will see, to establish Linkage early on and to always conclude with Plans. You will also see as you experiment with this model, however, that you will need to constantly identify Obstacles and Opportunities and repeatedly establish or renew Linkage, no matter where you are in dealing with a particular leadership or business challenge.

Throughout *Leading Innovation* we're going to show you how to keep the people you lead in the loop. We'll show you how to:

- Create Linkage. Help the people you lead to understand your organization's business challenges, the roles they can play in achieving your most important objectives, and the benefits – for themselves, you, the organization, and your customers – of taking responsibility for contributing as much as possible to create the innovative solutions for dealing with those challenges.
- Assess and address the Obstacles. Identify obsolete policies and procedures, resource issues, mindsets, behaviors, and other factors that are inhibitors to innovative performance.

- Generate creative Opportunities for changes and improvements. Make operations and business practices support, not block, innovation.
- Make Plans and build commitment. Get people to identify and tackle what needs to be done to make innovation a way of life for your team, department, or entire organization.

The elusive "simple" answer

LOOP Leadership has proven to be a wonderfully useful model for guiding the leaders and teams we have worked with over the years. We've used the LOOP Leadership Model in our work with organizations throughout the United States and in Europe and Latin America. We need to acknowledge a paradox, however, before we get too far into explaining why and how this tool can be so effective at tapping into the passions, energy, and ideas of the people you lead.

LOOP Leadership is not *the* answer. It is no holy grail. And yet, here we are, suggesting that learning and using LOOP Leadership can change your life and dramatically change the team you manage. It can – but not because it's formulaic, and certainly not because it's easy.

Gertrude Stein, the American author who gained notoriety influencing the artistry of the likes of Ernest Hemingway and Pablo Picasso, once said, "There is no answer. There never was an answer. There never will be an answer. That's the answer."

Some people draw a sense of hopelessness from these words, but this is one of our favorite and most inspiring quotes.

There *is* no single answer to any of life's complex challenges. To believe otherwise is a sure course to disappointment and frustration. The method you use today to resolve a critical conflict between your organization and a key supplier or customer may not work in a similar situation tomorrow. It might never work for a colleague in another company. Although it's imperative to build on our own experiences, and we can learn much from the lessons of others, it's rare that a solution used in one situation or used by one business can be plucked up and dropped successfully into another.

There is something that is even more detrimental to innovation than believing someone else's answer will work for you. It is believing that once you find an answer that works, you have reached an endpoint and can stop your search.

Colman McCarthy earned his international reputation as a syndicated newspaper columnist writing for the *Washington Post*. More recently, he has been active teaching peace and justice courses in law schools, universities, high schools, churches, and in community settings. We heard him describe an exercise he uses that makes a powerful point about the need for and value of continuing to challenge the status quo.

At the beginning of a course, he said, he sends the students out to the nearest busy street, instructing them to count the red cars and blue cars that pass by during a specified time period. When they return he asks, "Did anybody think that was a rather pointless exercise?" Almost without fail, he says, someone in each group admits, somewhat reluctantly, that the instant he gave the assignment it seemed like a bad idea. McCarthy's challenge: "Then why didn't anybody say so?"

Fear, uncertainty, complacence and many other environmental factors play a role in McCarthy's classrooms as clearly as they play a role in your organization.

Earl Bakken, co-founder of Medtronic, one of the world's leading manufacturers of pacemakers and other lifesaving medical devices, concurs about the need for risk-taking and questioning.

In his memoir, *One Man's Full Life,* Bakken says the scientific community tends to "think things to death, to demand too much 'proof,'" instead of focusing on innovation and creative thought. People are paralyzed by the need for statistical certainty. He says all this has meant missed opportunities for business and for humanity in general. He writes that, "Most of the good things in my life and career have come to pass because somebody was willing to rush in where more careful folks were afraid to tread."

To stop asking questions, to quest for and then settle for *the* answer, is to give up on change and innovation.

Leading innovation depends upon your willingness and ability to create an environment where questions are not only valued and respected, but also expected. The LOOP Leadership Model can guide the way.

Three hopes for leading innovation

As Kahlil Gibran's observation at the start of this chapter suggests, our work is guided by a deep belief that all people are uniquely talented and wise. It seems almost criminal when businesses and leaders, instead of finding ways to facilitate the use of that talent and knowledge, create systems that undermine individuals' own beliefs and confidence about their distinctive gifts. Sometimes the barriers are inadvertent. Sometimes they are more deliberate. In all cases, they are counterproductive to creating workplaces where people can soar.

We use the LOOP Leadership Model as a way to help organizations and their leaders foster the mindset and establish the management practices that truly tap into all the gifts people bring to the workplace. We also use LOOP to challenge the business realities that make us shake our heads in disbelief and dismay when we hear "employees are our most important asset" as words spoken but not values acted upon.

With all that in mind, we have three hopes for this book. We want to:

1. Raise your awareness about what it takes to create and foster an environment of innovation.
2. Stimulate your thinking about the innovations and changes you can make in your leadership style.
3. Provide a framework, models, tools, stories, resources, insights, and inspiration you can use to create your own unique action plans for leading innovation and creating a workplace where *your* people can excel, so *your* organization can thrive.

Remember, we're not promising any simple answers. No silver bullets. No formulas. No prescriptions. No step-by-step instructions. No scripts.

If we do our job well, we'll leave you with more questions than answers, and those questions will propel you toward an ever-evolving mastery of the art of innovative leadership.

Chapter 2
Innovate or Disintegrate

It is not necessary to change. Survival is not mandatory.

−W. Edwards Deming

Organizations that don't perpetually innovate and improve are on a course toward obsolescence. The speeds at which leading companies move forward into the future make status-quo-oriented competitors appear as if they are actually moving backward. But you already know this. You can feel it. It's a reality that has been keeping leaders awake at night for a long time.

- In the early 1990s Synectics Corporation surveyed 750 executives at 150 companies in the United States and found 80 percent felt innovation was critical to their company's survival, yet only 4 percent believed they were good at it. Years later, the problem persists at alarmingly high levels.
- In 2003, Boston Consulting Group conducted a similar survey with 236 senior executives in 30 countries and all major industries; 57 percent of respondents said they are dissatisfied with the return on the investments they have made in innovation.
- In February 2004, Deloitte, another global professional services and consulting firm, surveyed 650 manufacturers worldwide. In six years, Deloitte projects, 70 percent of what manufacturers sell will be obsolete due to changing customer demands and new competition. No wonder the respondents said that launching new products and services is their number one concern for driving revenue growth.

Peter Drucker, management guru, educator, and author puts it succinctly: "Every organization needs one core competence: innovation."

What these surveys and sentiments reveal, and what you are feeling, comes from four market drivers that no leader should overlook:

1. An organization's underlying market value is greatly influenced by its ability to innovate.
2. Innovation is the only sustainable competitive advantage in an ever-changing marketplace.
3. Future growth depends upon innovation.
4. Innovation is the means by which effective leaders make change occur within an organization – it is what fills the "white space" between what an organization has been and what it must become.

Innovation and market value

The bottom line on innovation – the word from the world's investors – is that companies noted for their ability to continually come up with new products and services are the best investments. Companies that best meet changing market needs or take markets in totally new directions are more likely to have long-term success and therefore are perceived as being worth more.

Fortune magazine provides compelling evidence year after year of the market value of innovation with its "Most Admired Companies" studies.

By all objective measures, General Motors is one of the world's largest companies. At last count, the car manufacturer has annual revenues of $195 billion, according to *Fortune*. In the 2004 Most Admired research it ranked fifth – *in the automotive industry* – and had an innovation score of 6.42 on a ten-point scale. Ford, the world's second largest publicly traded car company, has annual revenues of $164 billion. It ranked ninth in the automotive industry in the Most Admired research, with a 5.43 score for innovation.

Combined, the two manufacturers have a market value of $52 billion.

Microsoft, by comparison, has annual revenues of $32 billion. It ranked sixth *overall* in the 2004 Most Admired polls, and earned an innovation score of 7.67.

Alone, Microsoft has a market value of more than $288 billion, which means that even though it generates less than 9 percent of the total revenue of Ford and General Motors, investors give the software company a market value more than 550 percent higher than the two mega-carmakers *combined*.

Clearly, innovation is not the only thing that distinguishes these three com-

Top 10 Innovation Scores

Company	Revenue	Market Value	MV/R Ratio*
Washington Mutual	$18,629.0	$40,722.1	2.19
Starbucks	$4,075.5	$14,794.8	3.63
Procter & Gamble	$43,377.0	$134,678.1	3.10
Herman Miller	$1,336.5	$2,140.7	1.60
United Parcel Service	$33,485.0	$78,528.4	2.35
Nike	$10,697.0	$19,295.7	1.80
Fortune Brands	$5,912.5	$10,622.3	1.80
Newell Rubbermaid	$7,750.0	$6,969.8	0.90
FedEx	$22,487.0	$20,635.9	0.92
Pactiv	$3,138.0	$3,440.5	1.10
	$150,887.5	$331,828.3	2.20 (Cumulative Ratio)

Bottom 10 Innovation Scores

Company	Revenue	Market Value	MV/R Ratio*
Pride International	$1,689.7	$2,323.5	1.38
Fleming	$17,561.5	$66.5	0.00
Farmland Industries	$6,703.1	$0.0	0.00
US Airways Group	$6,846.0	$248.4	0.04
Cigna	$18,808.0	$7,871.7	0.42
Federal-Mogul	$5,546.0	$38.3	0.01
Kmart	$26,032.0	$2,694.2	0.10
UAL	$13,724.0	$389.9	0.03
Tenet Healthcare	$14,582.0	$5,633.2	0.39
Allete	$1,728.0	$2,903.5	1.68
	$113,220.3	$22,169.2	0.20 (Cumulative Ratio)
	(In Billions of US Dollars)	(In Billions of US Dollars)	

Source: Fortune.com

*MV/R stands for Market Value/Revenue Ratio (outstanding shares X share price / revenue)

This table compares market value and revenue (in billions of US dollars) for companies with the top ten and bottom ten scores for innovation in *Fortune* magazine's 2004 Most Admired Companies study. The cumulative market value to revenue ratio for the top ten companies is eleven times higher than it is for the bottom ten, a clear indication investors are willing to spend more for companies known for their ability to continually come up with new products and services.

panies and determines their market value. But if you are trying to persuade stakeholders or influencers to commit to innovation, the bottom-line *Fortune* data is persuasive beyond just this one case.

If you compare the ratio of market value (the total outstanding shares multiplied by the share price) to revenue (the MV/R Ratio) of the ten most and least innovative companies in *Fortune's* 2004 Most Admired list, you will see that investors are willing to pay eleven times more for companies in the top ten compared to the bottom ten. And this is a pattern we have seen repeated for years.

In their analyses of what distinguishes the most admired companies from the least admired, *Fortune* editors point unmistakably to innovation. They recognize that a many factors contribute to a company making it onto the magazine's list of most admired companies. Strong management, a talented work force, a high-quality product, sound financials – all are important. "But to be genuinely admired," they say, "an ineluctable quality must be in the mix as well: a spark that ignites the workforce and allows the enterprise to respond readily to change. That ingredient is innovation, and all the top companies embrace it passionately."

Innovation and competitive advantage

Virtually every product or service can and will be copied, often in a different part of the world, for less money, almost overnight. Think "offshore outsourcing." The time you can stand alone in the market with a new product or service before a competitor enters the game with lower costs or new features is shrinking.

The forces of change in the marketplace – such as increasing customer demands, mass customization, rapidly changing technology, global competition, and a shift to the "knowledge-based" society – are intense. Even corporate giants can be brought to their knees almost overnight.

There are many well-studied examples. Consider IBM, which miscalculated the personal computer market. Look at Sears, which numbly ignored Wal-Mart as a competitor well into the 1980s. At one point, Microsoft considered the need to deal with Internet technology so unimportant that it was dangling almost invisibly on the end of its priority list.

Innovators must develop perpetually innovative, people-driven organizations. They must create, foster, harness, and apply the collective intelligence of the organization – the intellectual capital – to create competitive advantage. Only by doing so can they create unique "humanware" that is impossible to copy.

Innovation, the S-curve, and white spaces

In order to thrive, companies must grow, and in the knowledge era, growth is synonymous with innovation. As the Deloitte study shows, launching new products and services is the number-one driver for growth.

Chuck Knight, chairman of Emerson Electric Company, started leading a deliberate cultural shift in that company in the late 1990s. He recognized that the electronics manufacturing giant had done about all the profit-taking it could through cost reductions. He feared the company had become idea-limited and would be unable to grow, but finally, he came to understand that their focus on cost-cutting was what was in the way. In response, he started his cultural shift by using two-day "growth conferences" in each of the company's sixty divisions to generate ideas for new opportunities.

It was amazing, he told *Fortune*, "sitting in those conferences, looking at all these growth programs, and thinking, 'Why haven't we done this stuff before?' Well, we hadn't done it before because we didn't have the resources to do it. And we didn't have the resources to do it because we were pounding the shit out of profit margins."

Emerson averaged a 10.6 percent total return to investors from 1993 up until 2003. In 2003, that number was 31.1 percent, and at the same time the company's scores in *Fortune's* Most Admired surveys also increased. In 2003 Emerson's overall score amongst American companies was 6.84, with a score of 6.4 for innovation. In 2004, the overall score was 7.69, with a 7.23 in innovation.

Emerson's sales in 2003 were $13 billion. Its market value: nearly $27 billion.

In a world moving ahead at today's incredible pace, it can spell death for an organization to focus on cost cutting or moderately upgrading the status quo, even when the status quo includes quality products and services and a history of success. It's vital to be cost efficient, but businesses must learn to simultaneously and continuously grow through new products and services, new applications for existing products, and by penetrating or creating new markets.

S-curve graphs are a tool commonly used for understanding the evolution of a product, service, technology, or even an entire organization.

- The lower left portion of an *S*-shaped line represents the start-up stage, when investment is heavy, the idea is new, progress is relatively slow, and success modest.

- The steep central part of the line represents the period when the product, service, technology, or organization is operating at peak performance levels.
- The upper right portion of the line represents the phase when the entity represented by the line is beginning to taper off or decline in performance.

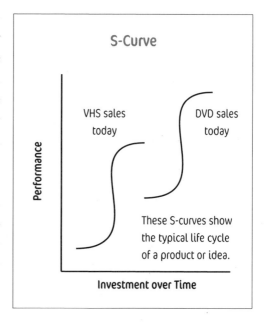

In the current marketplace, for example, the sales of VHS tapes of major motion pictures is moving into the upper right portion of the S-curve. Sales of DVDs, however, are on the steep incline because of superior technology, improved quality, high durability and reliability, cost competitiveness, etc.

When you position the S-curves as they are shown in the illustration – with the S-curve for DVDs to the right and slightly elevated above the curve for VHS tapes – the space between the upper right portion of the VHS curve and the lower left portion of the DVD curve represents the innovation or leap in technology that has occurred. It indicates the coming demise of VHS and the probable rise of DVD. At least for a while, before it too will reach its critical point.

What innovative leaders recognize is that this example represents a predictable and inevitable pattern for all their products and services and for every facet of how they do business. They know that the magic of innovation happens in the white space – the gaps between the S-curves, between technologies, between individuals or departments within a company – and it's their challenge to make something happen to bridge to whatever is next.

It won't be long before VHS tapes become nearly obsolete. They'll be in boxes with your eight-track music cartridges. But something new will also come along to challenge the market position of DVDs. It's already in the works. The challenge in leading innovation is to understand the curves and to work to stay ahead of them.

What's in innovation for you?

Revenue and market value numbers for companies change all the time, as do corporate reputations. Today's innovators, if they lose sight of the challenge of staying ahead of the product/service/technology curve, can quickly become tomorrow's also-rans. What doesn't seem likely to change, however, is that the innovators will continue to lead the way in the marketplace and be rewarded for that effort.

Change is the operative word in organizations today. It is coming at us from every direction. Change is imposed upon us from the "outside," but if we're wise we're making it happen ourselves from the inside, too. And it's a struggle either way. The editors of *Fast Company* magazine describe the pervasiveness of change in the marketplace this way: "It's not that the business environment is changing. Change is the business environment. And it's not that every company is undergoing change. Change has overtaken every company. Creating change, managing it, mastering it, and surviving it is the agenda for anyone in business who aims to make a difference."

That's what the marketplace place says about the importance of innovation. Before you ask how you as a leader can create an environment of innovation, however, you must first answer the question, "Why pursue innovation – in my team, my department, or my organization?"

You must find a compelling *business-related* rationale for innovation or your efforts will be perceived as a response to yet another management fad that, if people wait long enough, will go away like so many others. Do you need to dramatically improve service or quality? Is it critical you revamp your sales process to contend with web-based competitors? Do you need to build some extraordinary partnerships in order to grow and remain viable? Do you need to change from an available-product point of view and begin thinking instead about what the world needs that you can provide?

Innovation is enticing and exciting, but it is a means to an end, not *the* end, not the outcome. You must be able to evaluate your innovation efforts by hard measures. And those measures are unique in every situation. It is critical you get clear about what innovation will look like, specific to your circumstances, and what results will be achieved before you worry too much about getting creative.

Chapter 3
The Mental Breakdown of Innovation

At home, parents utter eighteen negative statements for every positive one – usually to an inquisitive child who wants to know how something works.

—CHARLES "CHIC" THOMPSON

Why is it so tough to lead innovation? A lot of the challenge has to do with lost genius.

The late Gordon MacKenzie taught us an exercise that demonstrated a powerful point about this. He was the author of one of our favorite books on creativity, *Orbiting the Giant Hairball,* and a longtime contributor at Hallmark Cards, where he gave himself the job title of "Creative Paradox" in his last leadership position. The last time we saw him, he looked a lot like Gandalf, the long-haired, gray-bearded wizard from *The Lord of the Rings* – except he was wearing luminescent multicolored parachute pants and leaping off chairs on a stage to make a point about risk taking.

In that same appearance, he posed this question to an audience of 500 executives: "How many of you in this room are geniuses?"

He looked around the hotel ballroom for a few long seconds, searching through the fidgeting group and listening through the nervous laughter for a single hand or voice to emerge. When he got no response, he suggested wryly that he would look around the room one more time, make eye contact with each person, and allow them to acknowledge their genius by giving him some secret sign – a slight nod, a wink, a small hand gesture. The result was another round of fidgeting and more laughter, yet no admissions of genius.

His point: Although the world is blessed with only a few Da Vincis and Mozarts, each of us is born with unique talents and gifts. But we tend to undervalue them when we compare ourselves to those we admire as "true geniuses." As a result, we tend to under use what makes each of us special. We settle for being safe and sacrifice most opportunities for being inventive.

Believing we lack creative potential is more than just a misperception – it has become a conditioned response. George Land, a noted researcher and author in the field of creative performance, created an assessment during the mid-1960s while working at NASA. The assessment determined which of the engineers and scientists was most creative. The instrument was quite predictive of people's success at NASA as innovators.

After using the assessment for several years, he became interested in the question of whether creativity was a result of nature or nurture. Were people born with an innate creativity or was it learned? To help answer this question he conducted a longitudinal study beginning with 1,600 five-year-old children.

Land found that at age five 98 percent of the group tested in the very high category of creativity.

He surveyed the same group of kids again at age ten and the number who tested as highly creative dropped to 30 percent.

By the time the group reached age fifteen, the percentage of those who tested as highly creative had dwindled to 12 percent.

Unfortunately, the decline in creativity does not end there. Land went on to test over 280,000 adults since the original study and found that only 2 percent of

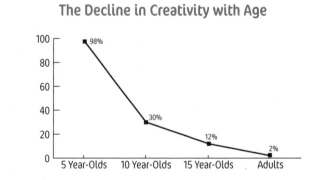

Research started in the 1960s by George Land shows a dramatic decline in creativity as people age. At age five, 98 percent of those he studied demonstrated high levels of creativity. By age 15, only 12 percent of this same group tested as highly creative. Further research with an additional 280,000 people showed only 2 percent of adults in the general population are highly creative.

adults in the general population scored in the very high category of creativity. Land's conclusion: *Non-creative* behavior is learned.

How does this happen? Mom and Dad tire of answering questions. Schools require coloring between the lines. Employers prefer hired hands who can be plugged into the mechanics of an organization to hired heads who might challenge smooth operations. We get socialized to conform. Our innate curiosity is replaced by a mental box into which standardized education is poured.

The good news here is that most of that creative genius isn't gone, it's merely repressed, or saved up for activities outside of the workplace. If we could continue to learn, fail, unlearn, and relearn at the rate of a five-year-old, our genius would reemerge.

So, leading innovation in your work team is very much entwined with your ability to reconnect with your belief in your own creativity. And it's dependent upon your ability to help the people you lead also to reconnect with their confidence in their unique talents.

Creativity vs. innovation

The words "innovation" and "creativity" are often used interchangeably. That can cause problems because, with some people, creativity carries a negative stigma in the workplace.

Creativity, to some, seems applicable only in the domain of artists, poets, and other "non-business" types. It implies risk-taking, rule-breaking, and unstructured chaotic activities that make some leaders extremely nervous. We don't happen to agree with those fears, but we suggest you avoid the potential problem by distinguishing between the two terms this way:

Innovation is the value-added application of a creative idea.

Think of innovation as being required by change but fueled by creativity. We have worked with people who are veritable fonts of creative ideas but fall short when it comes to acting on the ideas in ways that add value. Others struggle to innovate because their well of ideas has run dry. Innovation requires both the generative process and the value-added action. Note that we didn't say "good" ideas, "useful" ideas, or "practical" ideas. Indeed, one of the problems we have seen is the inability of some people to make a distinction between good ideas and bad.

Joyce Juntune, a professor and researcher at Texas A&M University, offers her "three Us of innovation" as a litmus test for determining if an idea has practical merit. Ask yourself if the idea is:

- Unusual. Is the idea new or uncommon? Is it unique?
- Understandable. Do others "get it?" Is the idea clear and comprehensible? A great idea is likely to languish if it can't be communicated or understood.
- Useful. Can you put the idea to work? Does it have the potential for solving a problem? Can it create some new opportunities?

Monumental, incremental, and elemental innovation

So, what does it take to create an environment that nurtures thinking that leads to ideas – ideas that are unusual, understandable, and useful?

First, it requires broadening the way you define innovation. Innovation is typically divided into two categories – monumental and incremental – but we add a critical third category. And we suggest that to build an atmosphere that re-covers that lost genius we talked about earlier, there needs to be a *mental* break-down in how you define innovation.

You've got to focus on and value innovation that is monu*mental* as well as in-cre*mental*, but most importantly, you've got to ensure that innovation becomes ele*mental*.

The *monumental* piece of innovation relates to dealing with the big stuff, the breakthroughs, the radical, new-to-the-world ideas. These are the major-payoff ideas that make the headlines. These are rare but extremely valuable innovations.

The *incremental* piece of innovation is focused on the small changes – con-tinuous improvements that make processes, products, and services just a little bit better. Some people have a knack for simplifying or modifying procedures or adapting other people's ideas in unique ways to different problems. These are the hundred-dollar and thousand-dollar tweaks that add up over time, but don't al-ways get much recognition.

One of the most important lessons coming out of the Total Quality Manage-ment movement that rolled across the globe from Japan in the 1990s is that in-novation is not only the big stuff. To thrive, your team and your organization need players who can come up with *monumental* improvements and players who can make *incremental* changes. Those may not be the same people, and their ac-complishments may not seem to be on the same scale, but you can make a huge step toward leading innovation by making sure you value and celebrate both.

That recommendation ties closely to the most important lesson about the mental breakdown of innovation: you need to lead in a way that draws ideas and energy from everyone, everywhere, everyday.

You've got to make innovation *elemental.*

You're going to have to get over any fears you may feel about encouraging people to be creative. You're going to have to let go of needing total control. You've got to foster a climate that values ideas for improvement that come from every corner of your organization, every day, in every facet of your operation. You can't lead innovation by handing an assignment to the research-and-development team alone or by sequestering your management group for a weekend retreat.

The never-ending and imperfect quest for innovation

Sections 2 through 5 of *Leading Innovation* will get into the details of how you can bring the LOOP Leadership Model to life and how to make innovation elemental to your organization's operations. Much of what you will learn is drawn from lessons discovered by leaders in organizations that are chasing innovation vigorously. One thing they each have figured out is that the pursuit of innovation is a race with no finish line. What – and who – is innovative today may be outdated tomorrow.

By the time this book reaches your hands, some of the companies held up for admiration on these pages may have stumbled. Enron Corporation is a classic case. It was a darling of the business media for years, praised from every direction as an innovator in the energy industry, and highly valued for its return to stockholders. But the company, its history of success, and its reputation crumbled overnight as a result of its accounting scandal. On the individual level, a client of ours talked recently about the promotion – and innovation devolution – of one of the company's top manufacturing-plant managers. He was elevated into an executive position in corporate headquarters precisely because of his willingness to try new things and to constantly improve operations. But in his new position, the plant manager began showing worrisome signs of being far more conservative when he found himself closer to the established power structure at the top of the organization. These lessons teach us that even where others have made a mess of things, there is still much to be learned.

We assure you, nobody leads innovation perfectly. You will make mistakes, stall, and falter. Everybody does, and that's part of leading innovation. Even in the exemplary companies, it's easy to find pockets large and small where people would refute their company's reputation for innovation based on their own experience within the company. The opposite is true, too. There are stodgy bastions of stereotypical corporate hierarchy where a single brave soul or a small core group is adding new spice to the company soup, and will one day get to share that recipe with the head chefs (who will probably take credit for it).

We're selecting our examples – good and bad – and keeping our advice at a level that will be valuable to you as an individual leader. We aim to help you, no matter whether you manage a team of one or one hundred. Or whether you are a lone voice for innovation in your organization or part of a large choir. Or whether innovation is part of your DNA or you dread the prospect of grabbing the status quo by the lapels and giving it a good shake for the first time in your life. We won't hold up any companies or individuals and urge, "Do exactly the same thing." As we've already said, that doesn't work.

Our hope is that you can use the lessons here to build your own innovation leadership strategy. We'll share the best stories and advice we have for this moment in time. They'll change. We're talking about innovation, after all. But each piece is a building block that can contribute to you becoming a shining star in leading innovation in your team, your department or division, or throughout your entire organization.

LINKAGE – CONNECTING PEOPLE, PROCESSES, AND PROFIT

Chapter 4

The Power of Choice

*There are actually no such things as "skills." There are only skilled people.
And people – as inconveniently human as they may be – are what make any
organization a success. Leading them, nurturing them and maximizing their
potential are any company's real core competency.*

–LENNY LIEBMANN

LINKAGE – The Linkage phase of LOOP Leadership strives for two outcomes critical to innovation:

1. Help people understand your key business challenges and how their roles tie into dealing successfully with those issues.
2. Help people establish for themselves why they should take ownership for your team's or organization's key challenges.

There is nothing more vital to innovation than the power of choice. You choose to lead in a way that fosters innovation – or not. The people you lead buy into – or do not buy into – your need for them to play a role in changing and improving the way you work together. And they choose whether to play those roles with all the talent and energy they have or merely to go through the motions, contributing just enough to keep their jobs.

Why is choice so powerful? Because organizations don't innovate. Companies don't create. People do. And if people don't choose to make innovation happen, it won't. The cycle of organizational innovation, from demand to fulfillment, results from the continuous interplay between the marketplace, your organization, and the individuals you employ, operating as a three-tiered, inverted pyramid, which balances on the precarious point of individual choice and performance.

At the top of the inverted pyramid are the customers and the marketplace. They constantly demand that your company offer more choices, faster delivery times, customization, sexier options, better technology, brighter colors. You know the routine: Change, change, change. They want everything bigger, better, faster – and cheaper.

You and your organization are the middle tier of the pyramid, wisely and proactively embracing the challenge the ever-changing marketplace provides. In response, you reorganize, merge, acquire, centralize, decentralize, outsource, institute Six-Sigma, lean manufacturing, or do both – "lean-sigma," etc. You know that this evolving demand from the marketplace is your opportunity to grow your business. You make the promise that whatever the customers want, your organization can provide. You have to, or else your competition will.

The promise can only be fulfilled, however, when the individuals who support the whole inverted pyramid, who together *are* your organization, embrace

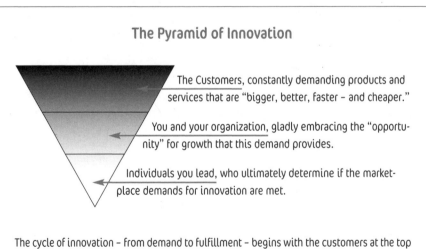

The Pyramid of Innovation

The Customers, constantly demanding products and services that are "bigger, better, faster – and cheaper."

You and your organization, gladly embracing the "opportunity" for growth that this demand provides.

Individuals you lead, who ultimately determine if the marketplace demands for innovation are met.

The cycle of innovation – from demand to fulfillment – begins with the customers at the top of the pyramid. Organizations on the lookout for ways to sustain and grow their business readily embrace demands from the marketplace. But the focal point upon which the entire structure balances is individual performance. That is why the power of people enthusiastically choosing to buy into the work required for innovation is so vital to a leader's success.

Exercising Choice

We use this quick Linkage exercise to dramatically and energetically demonstrate the power of choosing to engage and how Linkage helps ensure success. We've used it with groups with as few as eight people and as many as 500. It has never failed.

- Ask everyone in the group to stand.
- Instruct them to walk around your meeting space and greet their co-workers, acting as if they have no interest in them, and as if they have far more important things on their minds.
- Stop the group after approximately thirty seconds. Congratulate them on their skill at demonstrating apathy.
- Now ask them to continue walking and greeting, but this time to greet people as if they were long-lost friends.
- Stop the group after about a minute.
- Debrief the exercise by posing these kinds of questions rhetorically or by actually discussing them with the group: If you had the choice of working with group A (apathy) or group B (energy) which group would you chose to work with? Why? Which group has greater potential for success? How would you prefer to approach a challenge – apathetically or energetically?

We've done this exercise countless times since first learning a variation of it from Ken Blanchard. It is always an energizer, and it highlights the difference between apathy and energy.

It's important to stop that first round of greetings quickly, to avoid putting everyone into a permanent funk. Stopping the group in this phase takes little effort. People are generally listless and quiet.

In the second round of greetings, especially with large groups, you may have to climb on a chair or table, wave your arms, or blow a whistle to restore order. It often takes a full minute or more to cut through the noise, backslapping, and high-fiving.

Even people who are uncomfortable going through this exercise "get it." Virtually each person can see what choosing Linkage, or making a commitment, can mean. Most of the work we do with groups involves us asking them to participate in dealing with the business challenge the company has asked us to address. We point out to people in our sessions that after this exercise, they will have choices to make. They must choose how actively they will participate during our session. They must choose how committed they will be in implementing ideas and strategies created during our time together, after they return to their regular jobs.

Of course, much more goes into actually making and acting upon the choice to commit than merely understanding the potential power of that decision. That's what makes Linkage, the first component of the LOOP Leadership Model, such an important and difficult challenge in leading innovation. Using a variation of this exercise to fit your circumstances can be a great way to kick off an important discussion about how to make significant changes and innovations in your team or organization.

the challenge of delivering what your company intends to provide.

We've witnessed situations, and so have you, where two people working side by side, doing essentially the same work, choose to see the meaning of their work very differently. One worker sees her job building neonatal respirators as "helping to save the lives of premature babies." A colleague at the next station considers himself a "tube hooker-upper."

Your challenge in leading innovation, of course, is to create a workplace with as many lifesavers and as few tube hooker-uppers as possible. There was a time when organizations were designed with tube hooker-uppers in mind as the ideal employees – replaceable, compliant, cogs in the machinery. Although we know that mindset hasn't been totally wiped out in some parts of the business world, we also know you wouldn't have read this far if you believed that that formula fostered innovation.

Ten leadership strategies for building commitment

You can't flip some switch for people to make them see themselves more like lifesavers than tube hooker-uppers. But you *can* lead in a way that makes your workplace environment conducive to people making that choice for themselves. You can create an atmosphere in which choosing to be a lifesaver feels right for most of the people most of the time.

How? Here are ten strategies our clients find useful:

1. Constantly speak to the *value* of the work you and the people you lead do. What difference does your work make to the customers and others within the organization? There is plenty of evidence that one of the most powerful job motivators is meaningful work. What is the meaning of what you do? Can the people you lead feel this? Would they describe their work as meaningful? Meaningful work has a cascading effect – from you to those you lead and ultimately and most importantly to those they serve.
2. Involve people early and often in changes that substantially affect their work.
3. When involving people in decisions and changes, be clear about the type and level of input and involvement you are seeking. Nothing breeds cynicism more than leaders who've already made a decision but go through the motions of asking people for input to create a façade of pseudo-involvement. Be straightforward. Are you simply looking for their insights about some poten-

tial options you are considering? Do you want to involve them in brainstorming potential options? Who will make the final decision?

4. Give people options whenever possible – in matters big and small.

5. Provide continual updates on how you and the organization are doing compared to the stated objectives. People want to know if they're succeeding.

6. Give them control over as much of their own work as possible. Tell them what needs to be done but not how to do it.

7. Create the expectation that when people in your team come to you with problems, they need to also offer their own potential solutions.

8. Push as much of the decision making as close to the team members as possible. People own their own decisions much more than those imposed upon them. Teach them wise decision making.

9. Delegate as much of the important work as possible. It helps people learn and grow, feel more a part of the process, and gain a broader perspective on your business.

10. Ask for and act upon people's ideas and opinions. This does not mean you need to implement every suggestion. But every suggestion deserves a response, even if it is a "no" and an explanation why you won't or can't act on a particular suggestion. If ideas end up in a black hole, they will stop flowing.

Linkage is your invitation for the people you lead to get involved, full throttle, in making your organization more successful. It's your invitation for them to become life givers, if you will, in the process of creating and innovating.

As you'll see in the next two chapters, making that invitation irresistibly enticing begins with your being clear about your mission, vision, goals, and objectives – and about your ability to create connections between the people you lead and the work that must be done.

Chapter 5

Communicating Vision and Priorities

This "telephone" has too many shortcomings to be seriously considered as a
means of communication. The device is inherently of no value to us.

—Western Union internal memo, 1876

Communication technology changes at warp speed. Imagine what the tunnel-visioned Western Union memo writer of 1876 would say about today's Internet-ready camera phones, not to mention whatever high-tech gizmo is coming next. But while communication technology changes at a dizzying pace, the essence of true communication remains constant. The core of communication is connection.

When we talk about **Linkage** in the LOOP Leadership Model, we're talking about connection that goes far beyond the electronics of phone signals or the physiology of sight and sound bouncing off retinas and eardrums of people in the same room. The main objective of **Linkage** is to create a broad-reaching sense of *ownership* of what your organization must accomplish. That's because no single leader, no matter how creative or experienced, can innovate with the power, efficiency, or effect of a team of highly engaged stakeholders focused on making things better. The connection we're talking about, this sense of ownership, translates into commitment, passion, and personal investment, all of which are secured at a much higher price than simply circulating a memo or making a speech to introduce top management's latest-greatest success strategy.

Linkage is a vital early step in putting people on a track toward innovation or in beginning new projects. Your role is to help people establish for themselves how and why they need to be involved. This kind of connection begins with your ability to communicate a clear message about the work that has to be done. It culminates with your ability to help people come up with compelling and inspiring answers to the question, "What's in it for me if I put my heart and soul into making this change or improvement happen? Why should I be innovative?"

Linkage helps you establish the benefits for people who choose to actively learn and do what is necessary to accomplish desired results. It lifts the responsibility for the challenge off your shoulders – as "the boss" – and shares it with everyone, giving you an exponential increase in creative brainpower.

Medtronic co-founder Earl Bakken says what many leaders say about this challenge: Communication is one of the most important leadership responsibilities. As you well know, that's easy to say, harder to do. But he built his reputation as a globally successful innovator and industry leader by taking this responsibility seriously, speaking candidly, and insisting that others do the same.

In *Reflections on Leadership,* a collection of essays he wrote for Medtronic's fortieth anniversary, Bakken notes, "Leaders are only as good as they communicate, because without effective communication, any grand plans, bold strategies, or ingenious tactics are lost before they can persuade and encourage the very people who need to know them most – the employees."

He also warns that information too often is needlessly restricted to management, arguing that employees need to know how their daily work fits with the company's product or service, its overall strategies and plans, its problems, and its successes. It's worth risking such open communication, however, because "Inadequately informed, our employees are operating in the dark, or at least in a murky half-light, and thus susceptible to misinformation, misunderstanding, distrust, and resentment. If *we* [leaders] don't answer their questions, someone else will, and we may not be very pleased by either the source or the answer."

You've got to get people clear about what must be done and why, and you've got to get them to own the challenge. Neither task is simple.

How to communicate for connection

Our advice may seem painfully obvious, but the longer we work with organizations, the more we realize just how difficult it can be for some leaders to take care of the most fundamental management tasks. Common sense isn't always common practice – and we've heard a million different rationalizations why some leaders don't get around to communicating specific business challenges to the people they lead. None of these rationalizations undo the damage that limiting the flow of information causes.

The people you lead need to know three key things to perform well:

- Your company's specific goals and objectives,
- Your priorities for accomplishing those goals and objectives, and
- Your priorities for what they should be or are doing to help achieve those results.

They should be able to tell you, in their own words, exactly these three things. In particular, they should be able to describe how what they are doing right now links to the bigger picture. Try walking around and casually asking members of your team to do this, as a diagnostic on the effectiveness of your own communication. In our experience, the results are usually quite humbling.

The days of command and control management are, thankfully, mostly a distant memory. We know there are times when even the most enlightened leaders still wish they could say, "Just do this. Don't ask questions." But as a long-term strategy with a focus on innovation, it won't work. You must talk about and link your group's goals and priorities with individuals' daily tasks, regularly and consistently – in staff meetings, with project teams, in one-to-one performance discussions, standing around the water cooler. It's not an event; it's an environment, a condition, and a context for their daily decisions and actions.

Unfortunately, it is increasingly common for us to meet people frazzled by their workloads, frustrated by their inability to do anything more than take care of basic duties. Worn out by feeling locked into an unending cycle of having too much to do with too little time, they will numbly focus on the task at hand.

Surveys conducted in the US around the year 2000 point to some troubling trends. Productivity and revenue numbers were up, but employment statistics were down – more people were unemployed, and there was little job creation. Employees in all industries were feeling the pressure of doing more with less. As a result:

- 77 percent of workers were still going to work when they were sick, mostly driven by concerns about workload;
- 55 percent were feeling overwhelmed by their workload; and
- 45 percent were saying they would leave their current employers in five years or less.

None of these circumstances bodes well for creating connection or fostering innovation. In these situations, we have observed that much of the work force's creativity goes into figuring out merely how to survive emotionally – or worse, how to "beat the system" (it's also known as figuring out how to get paid as much as possible for doing as little as possible).

Looking for a remedy with one particularly stressed-out group of middle managers selected for a leadership development program by their bosses, we asked them to identify their top three to five job priorities. Then we asked them to list all of their typical daily activities. Finally, we asked them to match those activities to their top priorities. In this group, no one could narrow a list of priorities to only five, and the typical tabulation of activities looked like a grocery list for a hungry family of twelve.

These managers were unable to focus on their top priorities for one of three reasons:

1. They had never asked their leaders – nor had their leaders volunteered – to spell out top business priorities.
2. They had asked their bosses to spell out top priorities, but the bosses were unable to clearly delineate them because of a lack of clarity and priority farther up the chain of command.
3. They had asked about top priorities, learned there were enough to make several lists of five, and came away feeling frustrated, as if all those priorities were critical and not one could be neglected in any way.

It was clear that none of the participants in this leadership development program were satisfied with their own performance, nor were they thrilled with their work conditions. We strongly encouraged each of these people to sit down with their bosses to resolve the situation.

Over the course of several weeks' work, it became clear that few in the group had taken our recommendation. The explanations were numerous, but the common theme was that they and their bosses were too busy to make time to figure out why they were too busy. They weren't innovating. In fact, they consistently reported that they felt as if they were barely staying ahead of the next crisis.

Less than three months after the leadership program ended, more than half of this group was terminated in a "strategic" reorganization. Keep in mind that these managers were selected for this development opportunity because they were all seen as high-potential performers. But pressures were mounting and many failed to adjust. With better Linkage, the percentage of those who would have been considered contributors worth keeping on would have been higher.

Priority Assessment Tool

Here's a tool to help the people you lead see how their daily activity supports top goals and priorities. Ask them to write key words that identify either your or their top three to five priorities on the diagonal lines. Then ask them to list their current projects and responsibilities. Finally, ask them to assess which priorities (if any) each of their current activities actually support. Use the tool to clarify goals and priorities, and discuss whether activities that don't support priorities are worth doing now, later – or ever.

Current Projects and Responsibilities

	Priority 1	Priority 2	Priority 3	Priority 4	Doesn't support any top priority
_____	❏	❏	❏	❏	❏
_____	❏	❏	❏	❏	❏
_____	❏	❏	❏	❏	❏
_____	❏	❏	❏	❏	❏
_____	❏	❏	❏	❏	❏

Keeping it simple

The critical lessons for leaders creating Linkage are simply stated: Make time to help people get clear about their own top three to five priorities in helping achieve your business objectives. Make sure they know what you are trying to accomplish and that they see specific connections between their own tasks and performance and the "big picture." This will focus performance on essentials.

It's important to restrict priorities to three to five, because there are limits to what one person can accomplish. We're all circus performers spinning plates on the tops of tall sticks. If the ringmaster shows up with more plates after we've just used our last stick, something's got to change before we can add another plate to the mix. An all-too-common response in the business world, however, is to crack the whip and say, "Find another stick." But with that mindset, it isn't long before plates come crashing down everywhere.

Depending on your own leadership role in your organization, you may also feel overwhelmed as your boss continually shows up with new dishware for you to spin. That can contribute to your own lack of clarity about priorities, which is certain to spill over to those you lead. If that's the case, you've got to ask for the same clarity from your boss that your people need from you. Only you know how many sticks you have and how many plates you can keep spinning. The same is true for the people you lead. The number is different for everyone. It's vital to Linkage, and ultimately to innovation and overall performance, that there is an opportunity to say, "Enough – we've got to reevaluate our priorities and how we are going to accomplish them."

Of course, most organizations have significantly more than five major business challenges to confront every day. We're not suggesting priorities numbered six and above don't matter or aren't truly important. But some things truly have to come first, or everything will eventually suffer. And often, once you successfully address one of the first five, you can move on to a new one.

This has clear implications for you as a leader. If you bring new plates to team members who have nothing left to spin with, you need to be able to agree on which old plates need to crash to make room for the new, or you need to design a new way to spin more plates.

At the end of the day, the people you lead won't feel very good about their contributions if they've spent big chunks of their time sweeping up the mess of the broken plates they couldn't keep balanced. They won't feel good about their situations if the message they hear is that *everything* is a top priority. People will spend their nightly commute wondering if they're winning the game. If the demand to keep all the plates spinning is relentless, and they are unable to determine if they're successful, then morale will plummet, performance will suffer, and innovation won't happen.

Communicating with personal commitment

Helping the people you lead to make the connection and creating the sense of ownership that translates into personal passion and commitment are the toughest parts of Linkage. The first step is to give people the chance to explore the question, "What's in it for me, our team, the company, our customers, and any other stakeholders – if I get fully engaged in dealing with our challenges as creatively and innovatively as possible?"

Most important, of course, is "What's in it for me?" A reply like "You get to keep your job" doesn't cut it.

We usually spend time very early in our sessions working in small teams and then as a whole group to answer this question. For example, in a group being charged to come up with creative ways to restructure the functional operations within their department, we ask the teams to work together to create a list of the benefits they see to making the restructuring as successful as possible. We ask the small teams to share and compare their lists, and then we ask, "Are there enough benefits for you to say 'Yes' to this challenge?"

If the answer is "Yes," we're ready to move forward. If the answer indicates any resistance or reluctance, we explore what's missing. We ask about what problems exist or what reservations people feel. There is no sense going through any more effort to design changes if, in the end, there is not enough personal incentive for people to follow through on the proposed modifications.

One of the most effective ways to earn commitment and passion, however, is to demonstrate it with your own behavior.

Maggie Hughes, retired president and chief administrative officer of Allianz Life Insurance Company of North America, says, "You need to provide clear direction to people and get their input. But respect, appreciation, doing 'the right thing' for all stakeholders, and compassion are also essential in creating an environment of innovation."

That philosophy was never more tested – nor more valuable – than when, as part of the executive management team responsible for operations, she oversaw the merger of two financial service companies, Life USA Insurance Company and Allianz Life Insurance, to create Allianz Life. She had been one of the early employees of Life USA, known as an entrepreneurial company and recognized because of its unique culture and innovative products. Allianz, one of the largest financial services company in the world, came into the deal as a "traditional business giant," she says.

One of Hughes' goals when helping to build the operations of Life USA originally was to implement a "corporate commune" that would foster uniqueness, innovation, idealism, and create a true sense of employee ownership – literally and figuratively. She believes the spirit caught on, in large part, because "the leaders really worked to know every person in the company and to put them in places where they could succeed and grow. We had so few people for the amount of work that had to be done, we had to do things this way. We had to go the extra mile to nurture people, but it paid off. The result was that we created new products in an old industry, and we assured individual opportunities were there for every employee owner. A high school graduate working her way through the ranks into a senior executive position was not unusual."

It is Hughes' experience that good things happen when leaders really care about the people they lead. "But you have to care at a personal values level." She demonstrated her care by mentoring an employee council to give a high-level voice to employee concerns and ideas for improving everything from products and operations to marketing and management. She encouraged a "step-in step-out" program that allowed people to temporarily trade jobs – and points of view. And she created "Mornings with Maggie," which allowed five to six employees at a time to accompany her through a normal workday for a few hours to experience the company from her perspective.

"They got to watch everything that was going on, including conflicts between vice presidents. It was totally open," she says.

Another example was when Hughes, along with the rest of the executive management team, intervened in a mandatory training that was being planned around "insider trading issues" just before Life USA began publicly trading its stock on NASDAQ. The traditional path would have been to train a dozen or so high-profile "key personnel" in such issues. But given that Life USA was an employee-owned company where, in the early years, every employee invested 10 percent of his or her salary in the company, leaders agreed everyone needed to be educated about what was considered insider information and how the market worked. She was adamant that training "key personnel" at Life USA include all 300 employee-owners.

"At Life USA, we created a high-performance environment because everyone was in the loop. We were an orchestra. It was just my job to conduct the symphony."

When the merger with Allianz occurred, Hughes' challenge was to help bring together three hundred managers from both organizations – "a mix of the traditional 'suits' and the entrepreneurs who didn't even own suits" – and lay out all the issues. "And there were about six hundred issues identified by employee task forces. Issues related to business, interaction, policies, management structure … anything you can imagine.

"Both cultures knew we needed to change and become something entirely new. Life USA was a 'cool' company, open, innovative. Allianz had a long, traditional history." Ultimately she believed that the new, bigger company could be as innovative as Life USA had been on its own, but would require institutionalizing some of what came naturally in the smaller organization.

"I had to deal with some personal biases about large conservative companies, but I knew Allianz had fabulous people. I knew there would be opportunities for them to share their wisdom. And I knew the entrepreneurs at Life USA had new ideas to share."

In any organization, she says, "Linkage is about teaching people that they can make things happen. You have to give them information. You don't talk about deals prematurely, but as soon as they are solid you let people know. My philosophy is that you ask everybody you know for help, and you tell everybody everything you know. You have to. Everything changes. Things move so fast that without a good base of shared information you can't have long-term success."

Caring and sharing

Tim Staley, a district vice president for the YMCA, agrees that caring and sharing is critical to Linkage.

"One of our core values in serving the community is caring, and the culture within the Y is that we care about the people who work with us. They are part of who we are. In fact, we've been criticized at times about giving people too many chances. But one of the things that attracts and inspires people to work with us is that the environment is so healthy, respectful, and truly team oriented. In some business situations, people always know who 'the boss' *really* is, even when they talk about working in teams."

That doesn't inspire Linkage.

Far more effective for Staley is making sure everybody feels like a major player.

"When I'm dealing with junior staff members, it doesn't do much for me to watch them work and say, 'I've done what you are doing.' That's never enough. Telling them that I cleaned toilets like them in the past doesn't help us connect.

What makes a difference is when I show them that I am still willing to do that today with them, if that's what needs to get done. Saying. 'I will help you get this done,' is better than saying, 'I'm proof that you can get through this.'

"It's not enough that I have done daycare programs in my facilities for twelve years, or that I have gone through the complicated process to license programs. What matters to that staff is that I spend time in the daycare . . . that I talk to the teachers about their day, that I sit on the floor and play with the kids. I can't do it all day long, but when I am in there it really makes a difference to prove that I am involved."

People see through leaders who are insincere in their efforts to create Linkage. But as Hughes, Staley, and others have found, workers in the loop rise in support for leaders they know are genuinely committed to connecting their personal success to the success of the organization.

Chapter 6

Tapping the Talent

If you want to work magic, just remember its real name is creativity. And creativity is PEOPLE.

—Dennis Hightower, Walt Disney Company

Magic happens in the workplace when people get a chance to do what they are good at and what they care about. One of the quickest and most effective ways for you to create Linkage – which helps people connect to and take ownership for your business challenges – is to tap into talent and passion. Help the people you lead align who they are with what they do. Then watch creativity, innovation, and performance surge.

Sound too soft?

Mihaly Csikszentmihalyi (pronounced *chick sent me hi*), a noted psychologist, author, and professor, has conducted decades of research with hundreds of thousands of people at the University of Chicago, Claremont University, and elsewhere. His findings say otherwise.

Csikszentmihalyi's numerous books include *Flow: The Psychology of Optimal Experience*, which studies the conditions that enable people to perform at top levels *and* feel satisfied about their performance. When people perform well with a sense of satisfaction – whether at work or at home – they often describe themselves as "getting lost" in their work. They become so entranced with what they are doing that they feel simultaneously serene and ecstatic. They lose their sense of time and are totally absorbed, consumed, focused, and energized by their efforts. He describes those moments of optimal creative performance as "flow." Interestingly, Csikszentmihalyi discovered that these moments of peak performance and satisfaction are possible in any endeavor. Being fully engaged in and satisfied with an activity is not an innate attribute of the activity itself. Flow oc-

Getting in "Flow"

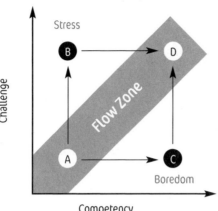

There is a natural relationship between competency and challenge that drives individual performance. If the level of competency (skill set, mastery, etc.) is appropriately matched for a given challenge, the person generally feels a sense of energy, focus, and motivation – all factors in creativity and innovation. (See point A.) This appropriate matching of competency and challenge is often referred to as a "flow" activity.

If a challenge exceeds the level of competency, a person will usually feel stressed (point B). It's also possible for the level of competency to outgrow the challenge, at which point boredom sets in (point C). To move back into flow from point B, a person must increase competency (learn new skills); to return to flow from point C, a person must find more challenging activities.

The types of activities that create flow are highly individual and change over time. Thus, ultimately it is up to each individual to direct the amount of challenge and learning that must occur to be satisfied and to perform optimally, but an effective leader will guide that decision making carefully and strategically.

TRY THIS
Use this model as a performance management tool.

Analyze the levels of challenge and competency related to key tasks handled by the people you lead. Consider how you can adjust the levels of challenge or competency they have to move them closer to "flow."

Adapted from *Flow*, by Mihaly Csikszentmihalyi

curs when the level of challenge is appropriately balanced with an individual's level of competence for handling the task at hand. Too much challenge creates stress. Too much competency creates boredom.

When you correctly match challenge with competency for those you lead, you set in motion a cycle of growth, discovery, energy, and creativity that is inherent in flow activities. Most people have an intrinsic desire to keep getting better at what they do and to avoid the stress and boredom that comes from being over- or under-challenged. Your job is to help people balance these two ends of the continuum. You need to support and encourage people as they step out of their comfort zones to take on progressively more difficult challenges or to develop new skills to reach their next levels of job satisfaction.

Keep in mind that the mix of activities, challenges, and skills necessary to reach new levels of performance and satisfaction is different for everyone, as is the rate of progress each person will make. One point of consistency, however, is that your job here begins with helping the people clarify what they are good at doing and what they feel most passionate about.

The T.O.P. Model of Creativity

How can you help people spend more of their working day in engaging and satisfying work?

Our T.O.P. Model of Creativity provides the guidance you will need to engage the hearts and minds of the people you lead and tap into the best they have to offer your organization. To do this you need to focus on three things: Talents, Open-mindedness, and Passion.

Talent

Talent. Play to peoples' strengths. Identify what each team member is good at and develop those skills.

That's logical, to be sure, but hardly common practice. Too much leadership effort is spent on getting people to fix their weaknesses. Unfortunately, many performance management systems encourage this practice. Even when 98 percent of the news from a performance review is praise for a job well done, it's far too common for people to focus on the remaining not-so-positive 2 percent. As Malcolm Forbes once said, "Too many people overvalue what they are not and undervalue what they are."

The T.O.P. Model of Creativity

This framework can help organize your big-picture thinking about what it takes to foster innovation in the people you lead, what it takes to engage peoples' hearts and minds. You must focus on three things:

Talent	Creative people figure out their strengths, gifts and skills, and they develop them and play to them. They leverage their strengths and manage their weaknesses, staying focused on what they can do, not on what they can't. Likewise, the most innovative teams recognize the value of having people with different strengths and personality types.
Open-Mindedness	Creative people are optimistic, opportunity oriented, and open to all possibilities. "Certainty" isn't a word in their vocabulary. Innovative thinkers don't change just for the sake of change, but they are willing and able to challenge everything.
Passion	Highly creative people are also extremely passionate about what they do. That involves aligning who they are with what they do. They understand the purpose of their work, and find meaning in it. They have fun, are challenged, and continually contribute and grow.

Think of each person you lead as having a unique combination of gifts and talents – a singular genius within each of them – that you can help them discover and use for making a unique contribution to your team or organization. People may be capable of doing anything, but they are incapable of doing everything.

Attempting to mold people into some image of excellence without taking their unique attributes into consideration leads to mediocrity at best, and frustrated discouragement at worst.

Ask top performers about their successes and they will tell you success happens when they are able to focus on doing what they do best. You will find that helping people develop their gifts is difficult enough. Trying to convert their weaknesses into strengths can be insurmountable.

The Value of Unique Gifts

This quote, from Marianne Williamson's book, A Return to Love, is one of our favorites for inspiring ourselves and others to acknowledge and appreciate our unique gifts.

Our deepest fear is not that we are inadequate. Our deepest fear is that we are powerful beyond measure. It is our light, not our darkness, that most frightens us. We ask ourselves, 'Who am I to be brilliant, gorgeous, talented and fabulous?' Actually, who are we not to be? ....Playing small does not serve the world. There is nothing enlightened about shrinking so that other people won't feel insecure around us. It is not just in some of us. It is in everyone! And as we let our own light shine, we unconsciously give other people permission to do the same. As we are liberated from our own fear, our presence automatically liberates others.

We are not suggesting that you make no attempt to help people improve in areas they are weak. Discuss and manage weaknesses or they will become liabilities. Weaknesses that remain blind spots inhibit top performance. But if you keep drilling into people's weaknesses you may never see their true gifts emerge.

One way to offset individual weaknesses is to use the diversity of talents within your team. Split duties in ways that allow people to spend most, if not all, of their time doing what they do best and enjoy most. Get clear about your overall objectives, and, as much as possible, divvy up the duties and responsibilities in ways that tap individual talents and passions. Imagine the potential of having every member of your team in flow. And when it happens, give out as much high praise, recognition, and reward as possible.

Identifying talents may seem daunting. It's part art, and it's part science, and it can get complicated and expensive. If you are part of an organization that has a training or human resources function, the experts in those areas probably have assessment tools you can use. Local college and universities as well as private consulting firms offer them, too. Or you can begin by simply sitting down with people and asking, "What are you good at? What do you love most about what you are doing? What do you want to do more of? What do you wish you could eliminate from your job description? How can we make that all fit with what we've got to accomplish together?"

It's critical, of course, that you ask these questions in a way that is non-threatening. People need to know you are not looking for reasons to get rid of them.

Talent Assessment Tool

Try this tool to stimulate discussions with people you lead. Ask: What are your talents? Use the list below to stimulate your thinking, but do not be limited by it. Add whatever terms best describe you. It may be beneficial to ask others who know you well to identify what they think are your greatest gifts. Then answer the question below.

Adaptable	Determined	Intelligent	Reflective
Adventurous	Diplomatic	Introspective	Reliable
Ambitious	Dynamic	Intuitive	Resilient
Analytical	Easy-going	Logical	Responsive
Assertive	Empathetic	Loyal	Risk-taker
Athletic	Energetic	Mathematical	Scientific
Balanced	Enterprising	Mature	Self-assured
Bold	Entertaining	Mechanical	Serious
Calm	Entrepreneurial	Methodical	Sincere
Caring	Expressive	Meticulous	Sociable
Charismatic	Fair	Motivated	Spontaneous
Clever	Flexible	Motivational	Strong
Clear Communicator	Focused	Objective	Systematic
Compassionate	Foresighted	Observant	Tactful
Competitive	Generous	Open-minded	Team-oriented
Concise	Goal-oriented	Optimistic	Tenacious
Confident	Handy	Organized	Thoughtful
Congenial	Hard-working	Patient	Thrifty
Considerate	Healthy	Perceptive	Tolerant
Cooperative	Honest	Persistent	Tough
Courageous	Humorous	Proactive	Trustworthy
Creative	Idealistic	Problem-solver	Verbal
Curious	Imaginative	Professional	Versatile
Decisive	Independent	Purposeful	Warm
Deliberate	Industrious	Quick	Wise
Dependable	Inspiring	Rational	Witty

In what ways are you – or could you be – tapping and developing these talents?

_____

_____

_____

Open-mindedness

Open-mindedness is critical for creativity, flow, Linkage, and the T.O.P. Model.

The most effective method for opening minds we've found is creating an environment where it is okay to question – and we mean question *everything*. You've got to create a workplace where questions are not only expected and respected, they are valued. Fostering a sense of curiosity and wonderment about possibilities becomes the driving force for continuous improvement, on an individual and an organizational level.

Charles Kettering was an auto-industry inventor who started the automotive parts company Delco, which he sold to General Motors in 1919. Throughout his career he was known as someone who was never satisfied with the status quo. He was always pushing for ways to change and improve products and operations. While he was part of General Motors, he had a running feud with a particular team of engineers about the length of time it took to paint their cars. At that time it took thirty-seven days, from start to finish. He wanted the time cut dramatically. The engineers said they thought they could cut it to thirty days. He scoffed and said one hour would be more like it, and then went on to develop his own fast-drying paint.

Later, Kettering invited one of the skeptical engineers to lunch at his plant. After eating and talking business, he walked the engineer to the parking lot, where he asked the engineer to point out his car. The engineer stood looking a bit confused, and then admitted he could not locate it. Kettering pointed to a vehicle parked nearby and asked, "Isn't that it right there?" The engineer replied that it was similar, but added, "My car isn't that color." Kettering, whose crew had surreptitiously painted the car during lunch, said, "It is now."

We realize that's quite a dramatic example of how to lead in a way that shows your commitment to open-mindedness. But sometimes drama does the trick.

A contemporary of Kettering's was Eldrige Reeves Johnson, inventor of the Victorola. He first marketed his groundbreaking record-playing machine in 1906, but evidently he shunned progress, and in 1921 the latest Victorola was virtually identical to the first models ever built. They weren't even electrified. And he ignored the competition and the change in technology presented by the invention of radio in the 1920s. In fact, the culture of his organization was described as sending a very clear message: Don't even use the word "radio" around here. The apparent "strategy" was to ignore change and innovation, but by

Christmas 1924, sales of the Victorola had slumped dramatically. The company was eventually bought in 1929 by RCA, which had no interest in the Victorola. RCA wanted the company's manufacturing plant and distribution network.

There's an adage that captures the difference in these two outlooks: *If you always do what you've always done, you'll always get what you've always got.* And as the competition increases, "what you've always got" may not be good enough to stay in business. So, you must set the tone in creating an open-minded environment in which everyone feels free to challenge your processes, procedures, and operations. Begin by scrutinizing what you do, asking why you do things the way you do and looking for ways to change and improve. Then ask others to do the same.

A simple step for fostering Kettering-like open-mindedness is to eliminate the word "certain" from your team's vocabulary, at least as it relates to creating solutions. As soon as you are *certain* you have a solution, the search for something better ends and your solution can become your biggest hindrance to further innovation.

Demonstrate that you are willing – and it is okay for others – to challenge everything, not in a complaining, critical, blaming way, but with an underlying sense that maybe things could be better. Questioning everything doesn't mean you will change everything, but it does mean you are willing to look with fresh eyes on old challenges.

We also recommend you regularly *challenge your assumptions* and encourage others to do the same. One client of ours, a catalog merchandiser, assumed that overhauling and streamlining its processes for producing marketing materials would eliminate a perpetual problem with missed deadlines and improve their creativity. So management instituted new process guidelines and standards. These new guidelines did solve the deadline issues, but it wasn't until a year later when they stopped to evaluate the output of their work that they realized the guidelines were hampering creativity.

The quality of the marketing materials was suffering, as was morale. A once-inventive team of writers, designers, illustrators, and marketing strategists assumed the guidelines couldn't be breached, so they stopped stretching.

It took an in-depth dialogue about the assumptions before it was possible to combine the efficiencies of the process guidelines *and* the creative potential of the group.

Passion

Passion is often the most difficult piece of the T.O.P. Model to address, but aligned with the power of choice, it can also be an incredibly potent force for change and innovation.

Why elevate passion as a catalyst for performance and as a measure of business success?

"We are in the twilight of a society based on data," says Rolf Jensen, director of the Copenhagen Institute for Future Studies and author of *The Dream Society: How the Coming Shift from Information to Imagination Will Transform Your Business.* "As information and intelligence become the domain of computers, society will place new value on the one human ability that can't be automated: emotion. Imagination, myth, ritual – the language of emotion – will affect everything from our purchasing decisions to how well we work with others." And, as Csikszentmihalyi's research demonstrates, emotion is a major component of flow and optimal performance.

If you have a hobby you really care about, you know what passion can mean. It feeds your desire to increase your mastery, whether it's related to playing golf, sculpting, gardening, singing, or collecting rare coins. You make time for this piece of your life no matter how busy you are with your other responsibilities.

You may be thinking the divide between passion at work and passion about life outside of work presents a gap that's too wide to bridge and lead anyone across. Not so.

Csikszentmihalyi's research shows that work, by its very nature, offers people greater opportunities to engage in challenging tasks that require a greater degree of their skills than the typical leisure activities they pursue. Thus, paradoxically, they have more flow experiences at work than at leisure. As a leader, your opportunity lies in figuring out what in your organization throws people out of their flow zones and getting them back into them.

Granted, some people will have trouble seeing across the divide and struggle to see how to bring their passion to their work. They may think only doctors, teachers, executives, or the Mother Theresas of the world have jobs that are truly meaningful and warrant passion. But we have all run across the hotel doormen, janitors, computer systems analysts, plumbers, venture capitalists, real-estate agents, police officers, factory workers, accountants, and shoe salespeople who are passionate about their work.

At a manufacturing plant in Arizona, we worked with a manager who struggled to see the connection between his life's passion – telling the story of his Native American heritage through film and art – and his everyday work overseeing the manufacture of computer discs. It was a co-worker who pointed out that, although he may not be producing films on the job, this manager was telling the story of his heritage every day through his every interaction in the workplace. This newfound link between the manager's ultimate passion and his everyday work immediately reinstilled an energy and zeal he had lost for his work and management style.

Don't let the people you lead perpetuate the misperception that meaning and passion are part of some jobs and not others. High performers and innovators bring meaning and passion with them wherever they go; they don't expect to have it handed to them on the way in the door to work. You have to help people tap into their passion and find ways of expressing it in their work.

Learn from your people what they are passionate about in life. What things matter most to them? Find out from them how much passion they believe they are bringing to their work. Get a rating on a one-to-ten scale. Then ask them how satisfied they are with that number. Ask them in what specific ways they are bringing passion to their work, and brainstorm what else they could do.

In creating Linkage, your message about innovation, involvement, talent, open-mindedness, and passion must be consistent and persistent. You've got to make it clear time after time that everybody wins with innovation, and you are willing to take some risks and tolerate some mistakes to make it happen.

It is always easier to play things safe, to do nothing new or out of the ordinary. Without your ongoing support and encouragement that is the path many people are likely to follow. But playing it safe doesn't lead to innovation.

Csikszentmihalyi says in *Creativity: Flow and the Psychology of Discovery and Invention* that all people are born with two "contradictory sets of instructions," one conservative and the other expansive and exploratory. While the instincts for self-preservation and energy-saving come from the first set, curiosity, creativity, and affinity for risk come from the second. And while our instincts for self-preservation require little if any reinforcement, our internal instructions for creativity and curiosity, Csikszentmihalyi concludes, require conscious cultivation and encouragement or else they are "easily extinguished," which is the subject of our next section: obstacles to innovation.

Lifeline Alignment Tool

People who bring passion to their work often have a clear sense of purpose about what they are doing and why. They have aligned who they are with what they do.

For some, identifying a personal sense of purpose is intuitive. They just feel it. They can't imagine their lives not doing what they do. For others, it takes more reflection.

Use the Lifeline Alignment Tool on page 57 for personal reflection and in performance management discussions to help yourself and others identify personal purpose and passion.

Imagine that the straight vertical line is your lifeline. It represents your life, as you would live it if you were 100 percent clear at all times about your purpose. If you could follow that path at all times, you would always be in flow, feeling inspired, challenged, energetic, satisfied, fulfilled, and creative.

In reality, however, we tend to follow paths through life that look more like the curved and wandering line that traverses the lifeline. Sometimes we live our purpose and feel engaged and alive in what we are doing, and other times we get away from the lifeline and feel disengaged and out of synch. The more misaligned we become, the more we feel bored, dissatisfied, empty, unfocused, and uncreative.

You can use this tool to help the people you lead identify times in their lives when they felt most positive about what they were doing and times in their lives when they felt least positive. Use this awareness to identify the jobs, projects, activities or moments when people are or were most and least closely aligned with expressing their talents and passions. Ask them to pay close attention to the moments of "flow" and make note of what is happening at those times. Then ask: What do the times of alignment have in common? What can you learn about yourself from those times? What can you do to increase those activities that feel more aligned with who you are? What are you "doing" when you are "being" truly who you are? What are the common elements of the times of misalignment? What can you learn and apply to your work and life to lessen those times?

Invisible assets of self-directed performers

Some people need little or no leadership when it comes to innovation. They require no prompting or guidance. They set in motion their own cycles of growth, discovery, energy, and creativity.

Life would be so much better – and leading innovation would be so much easier – if only we could figure out what it is that makes these self-directed innovators self-directed – and how to put that stuff in a bottle.

We've wrestled with this fundamental question for a decade, and we've come up with six characteristics – invisible assets – that we believe distinguish those

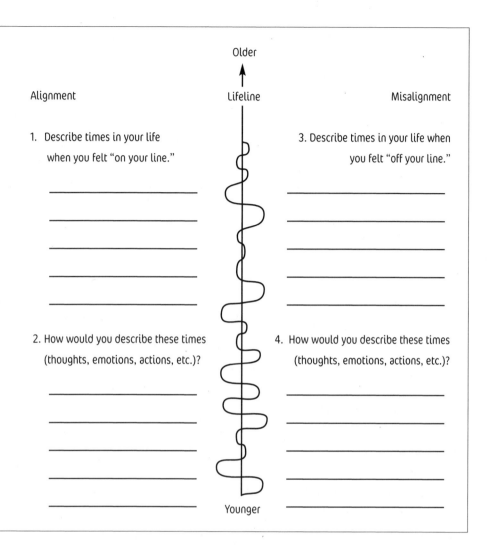

Older

Lifeline

Alignment

Misalignment

1. Describe times in your life
    when you felt "on your line."

3. Describe times in your life when
   you felt "off your line."

_____

_____

_____

_____

_____

_____

_____

_____

_____

2. How would you describe these times
   (thoughts, emotions, actions, etc.)?

4. How would you describe these times
   (thoughts, emotions, actions, etc.)?

_____

_____

_____

_____

_____

_____

_____

Younger

_____

who successfully take personal responsibility for their learning, careers, and motivation for making things better.

Here's what to look for and encourage. Self-directed performers:

1. *Work with an underlying sense of purpose.* The meaning of their work goes be-
    yond job descriptions. They're guided by passion that exceeds the narrow de-
    finition of tasks performed.
2. *Never surrender the art of dreaming and re-dreaming,* no matter how many

bills there are to pay or kids to put through college. Many people fail to set and achieve goals because they've lost the ability to inspire themselves. Dreams provide fuel and create direction.

3. *Focus on their gifts.* They know that attempting to become all things leads to mediocrity at best. Ask any top performers about their success and they will emphasize having focused on doing what they do best.

4. *See themselves as volunteers, not victims.* At the core of self-direction lies an internal locus of control. The self-directed take responsibility for their choices. They understand that any change in the direction of their future must begin inside them.

5. *Act despite their fears.* Uncertainty and change are inevitable, but being immobilized by them is not. Initiating action – any small action – sets into motion events that don't happen without the courage to begin.

6. *Thrive on interdependence.* All the benefits of self-direction can be lost in an organization or team unless self-directed performers master the art of interdependence. It's essential to trust, collaborate, and rely upon others. Success is impossible without interconnections.

Can this stuff be bottled? Can it be taught?

A better leadership strategy is to think of uncorking what already exists. Help people tap into their invisible assets. For some, that means identifying their sense of purpose, dreams, and gifts for the first time. For others, it means cutting through the fog that working for a living can create so they can once again see these characteristics clearly within themselves. With that clarity will come the courage and commitment to grow and innovate.

OBSTACLES – WHAT'S IN THE WAY OF INNOVATION?

Chapter 7

Myths and Methods

I have been through some terrible things in my life, some of which actually happened.

—MARK TWAIN

> OBSTACLES – The Obstacles phase of LOOP Leadership strives for two outcomes critical to innovation:
> 1. Identifying and overcoming whatever gets in the way of dealing with important business challenges in innovative ways. Policies, procedures, mindsets, behaviors, and operational practices – on an organizational and personal level – are fair game.
> 2. Examining and understanding the risks in not challenging the status quo. Being open to – and even inviting – change is the key.

A colleague of ours visited a community ice rink recently for a skating party with a group of friends. He came away not having skated and shaking his head, wondering what the leadership team that ran the facility could possibly be thinking in creating policies that kept him off the ice and resulted in him being a very unhappy customer.

The person who organized the outing spent a lot of money to reserve the rink for private use for one hour. Most of the group showed up with their own ice skates, but our colleague arrived planning to rent his from the facility. The two teenagers managing the operation that day, however, told him he could not rent skates to use in the rink his group was renting. He could, they said, rent skates and then pay a small amount to use in the adjacent rink, dedicated to "open" skating. They saw no incongruity in that situation, so he asked to speak with a manager. None was available. He asked if the teen workers could bend the rules on this one occasion. They apologized graciously but made it clear that doing so would put them at risk with the boss. It had happened before. So, the rental skates sat unused while he sat frustrated in the bleacher seats, watching his friends skate instead of skating himself.

We're confident there is an explanation for the policy that left this one customer skateless and many in the group thinking, "Next time we spend our money someplace else." But it wasn't offered. We're also confident the policy wasn't designed to anger buyers or to put teenage staff members in tenuous positions with customers. But it did. The teen staff members knew intuitively they weren't acting in the best interest of their customers, but self-preservation took priority over their concern for service quality. That's how obstacles work.

A LOOP-oriented leader would be engaging staff members in efforts to identify and eliminate or alter these kinds of obstacles and problems. It's obvious that wasn't happening here, at least not in this situation.

The obstacles in your organization may not be quite as obvious as being in business to rent skates but having policies that prohibit skate rentals. But you can be sure obstacles exist. Our goal for section 3 is to give you tools and ideas for identifying those barriers that may be inhibiting innovative solutions to your unique challenges. It's important to understand first, however, that there are some mindset obstacles to innovation that are widespread. In particular, we are talking about Four Myths of Innovation that are especially noxious.

Four myths of innovation

We have observed in our work with clients that many false myths seem to have supernatural powers of survival in organizations. There are four "biggies":

Myth #1 – Technology is innovation

Myth #2 – Innovation is only for artistic types, frizzy-haired scientists, computer geeks, bosses, and other "geniuses"

Myth #3 – All companies encourage people to be innovative and creative

Myth #4 – Innovation is a fad that will pass

Myth #1 – Technology is innovation

It's not. Innovation is the people.

There's no arguing that computer-driven technology, the beloved offspring of the industrial revolution, dramatically changes the way we work. But technology is not innovation; it is a product or outcome of innovation. In fact, technology levels the playing field between competing companies. It's an equalizer. But it is the *people* who develop and use technology who most distinguish competitors from one another.

The idea that technology is innovation is a powerfully misleading myth. Believe it and you'll probably agree with the pessimistic vision that the factory of the future will be a dark, windowless building, filled with computer-controlled machines and robots, and inhabited by only two living creatures: a dog and one human. The dog is there to make sure no one messes with the machines. The human is there to feed the dog.

We don't buy into that line of thinking. We have seen far too many "forecasts" of widespread job losses due to new technology be proven false in the long run. It is silly to believe that human ingenuity and input can ever become expendable.

Technology, innovation, and business are inextricably interwoven. Since the early 1800s at least, modern society has had a love-hate relationship with technology. From the start of the industrial revolution, writers lauded technology as the salvation of the common laborer. On the other hand, between 1811 and 1816, fear and distrust of mechanization went to an extreme, driving some British workers to riot and destroy labor-saving textile machinery. They were called Luddites, a term returning to common usage today to describe technophobes.

What would those anti-progressives say about technology today? Enthusiasm for new technology – for the World Wide Web, nanotechnology, biotechnology, genetics, robotics – is feverish. Rightly so. As we enter the new millennium, we are linked virtually to the entire world through technology, for better and for worse. We're continually refining the use of mechanics and digitization to create new jobs and eliminate old ones, improve old services and products, and essentially bring us into the realm of what once was considered fantasy. And more is sure to come.

It would be wonderful if technology or some process improvement could magically make an organization innovative, but it won't. The work of researcher Robert Kelley done at Carnegie Mellon University brings us back around to the importance of people and culture in the ability of organizations to innovate.

Kelley says, "It's a given that today's companies must keep new products and services coming – and respond quickly to continually shifting consumer demands. To maintain this competitive pace, managers need to improve the productivity of knowledge professionals. But while many have expected new technologies like company-wide computer networks to boost performance, the real promise lies elsewhere. Changing the way professionals work, not installing new computers, is the best way to leverage this intellectual capital."

We can use technology to create, gather, store, and manipulate information. Information can help us be bright, but information *isn't* knowledge. And knowledge *isn't* innovation. Innovation is what is done with that knowledge – how it is shared, built on, applied, questioned, and altered that leads to innovation.

Geoffrey Colvin, a columnist for *Fortune* magazine, says, "You must keep your infotech current with that of competitors – but for sustainable competitive advantage you'll have to look elsewhere. Where? The answer I'm hearing from executives around the world and in all sorts of industries is: in the most distinctively human elements of business – culture, leadership, character."

Technology has a potent influence in business, but with every step we take deeper into the knowledge era, it's clearer that successful organizations are coming to understand the importance of tapping the unique talents, skills, passions, and creativity that people bring to the work formula. John Naisbitt captured the essence of this important truth in a succinct phrase way back in 1988 in his eye-opening book, *Megatrends*: "High-tech, high-touch." The "tech" needs the "touch" of people.

Myth #2 – Innovation is only for artists, frizzy-haired scientists, computer geeks, bosses, and other "geniuses"

In today's knowledge era, success depends almost entirely on brainpower, a resource that post-World War II industrial organizations deliberately limited. That is, managers did the thinking; everyone else was expected to follow instructions. Creativity and control were reserved for the select few in the executive suites or the research-and-development or marketing areas. It worked. For a while. Demand was high, competition was limited, and change relatively slow-paced. Organizations could rely on these isolated pools of intellectual capital and still succeed.

That's not the case any more. The rules of the game of business have changed. They continue to change daily. The command-and-control, military-and-industrial model is broken, and if you are still using it to figure out how to keep up with the constantly and radically changing demands of the market, you are missing the most promising course to the future. You are missing out on a substantial portion of the intellectual assets of your organization. The only way to innovate perpetually is to unleash the cumulative intelligence, ability, and desire to be creative of your workforce.

It was a former field representative who – against normal industry practices at that time – was made part of the executive founding group, and who then pushed the leaders at Life USA to not only offer life insurance, but to provide annuities as well. That was a move that was innovative and groundbreaking for the industry, valuable for customers, and very profitable for the company, according to Maggie Hughes, former president of that financial services company. It was a McDonald's franchise operator, not the brain trust in corporate headquarters, who came up with the idea for the Big Mac, which was a revolutionary idea in the burger business at the time. And it will be a brave teenager, frustrated about being unable to rent skates to skaters at the ice rink, who will finally give voice to that problem and probably come up with a solution.

It is the people you lead who hold the potential for all innovation in your organization. John Mickelthwait and Adrian Wooldrige emphasize the need to tap this reservoir in their book, *The Witch Doctors*. "To harness [the knowledge in workers' heads], the manager needs to be able to understand it, define it, locate it, measure it, and encourage it to grow. Above all, the manager must be able to turn that abstract phenomenon into winning products."

Myth #3 – All companies encourage people to be innovative and creative
Most companies say they value innovation, but ask yourself how good you think your company is at putting actions behind the words. Our guess is that your response will be, "Not nearly as good as we need to be."

Recall the survey we referred to in chapter 1. We had the top managers in a 500-million-dollar division of a high-tech company ask employees if they believed the average worker in their organization had ideas that could help make the company more successful. More than 95 percent said, "Yes." We also had them ask if employees are regularly asked for those ideas. More than 95 percent said, "No." In another of our client organizations, one of the world's largest manufacturing companies, a telling employee satisfaction survey revealed that only 34 percent of workers felt management did a good job of acting on employees' ideas.

We'd like to believe these are exceptions to the norm, but our experience tells us otherwise. We've seen a widespread disconnection between what executives preach about innovation and the reality of what gets practiced and reinforced in the depths of organizations. The dangerous truth seems to be that we haven't totally walked out of the shadow of that industrial command-and-control model of management. We're battling against centuries of historical influence. It's going to take more than talk to show the people you lead you are serious about encouraging innovation and creativity.

Myth #4 – Innovation is a fad that will pass

Business people tend to learn some lessons slowly. Some leaders have a propensity for latching onto fads in search of easy answers to tough problems. Let us put it bluntly:

- Innovation is not a fad.
- Becoming more innovative is not a quick fix.
- Innovation can't be invoked through hollow proclamations from the corporate boardroom.
- Innovation is not an "event" or something you "do."

In short, *innovation is a way of being* – a mindset. It must be ongoing, and it must be woven into all facets of a business on the individual, team, and organizational levels.

Jim Champy, co-author of the influential book *Reengineering the Corporation*, pointed out a significant shortcoming of that book – after it had been on the market for about two years and sold two million copies. In his follow-up book, *Reengineering Management*, he said the trouble is that "popular concepts sometimes look like magic, and the more popular they become, the more powerful the magic seems. Some managers, misled by wishful thinking, believe merely repeating the key words in *Reengineering the Corporation* is enough to bring the transformation, like the newsboy in the comic strip who yelled 'Sha-zaam!' and became Captain Marvel." Of course, as Champy knew, this is not the case. His reengineering initiatives are long-term commitments, requiring continuous effort and more than occasional management lip service.

If ever there were a reason to avoid falling into the trap of turning a solid idea into the next "program of the month," your effort to lead innovation is it.

Change readiness – a major obstacle to innovation

Another common obstacle to innovation is a lack of "change readiness."

Remember the 1997 blockbuster film *Titanic*, starring Leonardo DiCaprio? There are several scenes that carry an important business message you might want to watch and then discuss with the people you lead. Use it as a starting point for a discussion about how ready, willing, and able you are as a team to handle the speed of change in today's business world and the need for growth and innovation.

The movie carries viewers back and forth between the present and the past. Scenes on a current-day salvage ship exploring the sunken *Titanic* are juxtaposed with scenes from the ship's maiden – and fateful – voyage. Early on, Captain E.J. Smith is handed a telegram on the bridge of *Titanic*, warning him there are icebergs along his course in the North Atlantic. He contemplates the message briefly, folds it and coolly orders his crew to light two more engine boilers in order to increase speed. Smith is confident that his vast sailing experience and the supremacy of this new ship will see them safely along their passage.

Everyone in the theater knows, of course, that Smith is wrong and that his mistake will tragically cost the lives of more than 1,500 people.

The business lesson comes when the film cuts away from the past on *Titanic* to the present on the salvage ship. With 20/20 hindsight, the captain of the salvage ship can see vividly that everything Smith knew about sailing and the sea was wrong. The marketplace had demanded bigger, faster, more luxurious ships, and the White Star Line had responded by building the "unsinkable" *Titanic*. Smith was handicapped by his twenty-six years of experience because, while sailing technology had changed, the sailor had not. Looking at things the way he always had, Smith did not account for the size, power, and ultimate vulnerability of this new ship.

That was 1912, and the inability to maneuver that new ship through old waters was catastrophic. Granted, few of us hold the lives of 2,200 people in our hands, as Smith did, by the nature of the work we do. But the risks are great for businesses charting courses in the new millennium based on old habits, outdated knowledge, and obsolete experience. The rate and magnitude of change, the demands of the marketplace, and the influx of new technology today dwarf what was happening at the beginning of the last century and will only increase in the future. The unsinkable ships in corporate America will be those able to travel at will – and at mind-bending speed – by air, land, sea, or fiber optics.

Today's leaders must have the ability and willingness to move beyond merely overcoming resistance to change or dealing with it. They must seize the opportunity and inherent power of the dramatic shifts in the marketplace. They must see the potential to invent and re-invent their own futures. They must foster in themselves and in others a mindset that keeps them constantly aware of and able to deal with ambiguity and to learn, unlearn, and relearn rapidly through their actions. We all must play the game of business with ever-changing rules, and be unencumbered by what is, so we can focus on what might be.

Paradoxically, organizations and people are least likely to change when they are in the best position to do so. The impetus for change is rarely great enough to overcome the inertia of the status quo until people and organizations hit a crisis (remember the S-curves in chapter 2?). Typically, change agents within an organization struggle to get the attention and resources for proactive change until the need to change is critical. Unfortunately, this is often a less-than-ideal time for change. Resources will be tighter. Some of the best people will have moved on out of frustration. Chaos will replace calm. Leading innovation requires a desire to work *with* – and to harness – the powers of change.

Charles Handy, the author of *The Age of Unreason*, *Beyond Certainty* and numerous other books, is among the leading business thinkers who have argued that it's no longer possible to draw a straight line from the past to the present and into the future. Things change too fast and too unpredictably these days. Handy says success will come to "the ones who look to the future, not backward, who are certain only of uncertainty and who have the confidence and ability to think completely differently." Change isn't gradual, it's constant and tumultuous.

Unfortunately, it's human nature to tenaciously hang onto the status quo. Until the pain of holding onto the old ways is great enough, it's always easier to do nothing than to face doing something new. That's why we stay in dysfunctional or dangerous relationships in our personal lives, why we hold onto jobs we despise, and why we stand by products and services that all indicators tell us need to change.

We don't know why Captain E.J. Smith failed to keep pace with change in seafaring. We do know, however, that each of us faces the same kind of challenge to continuously learn and grow, or suffer the consequences.

Preparing people for change

Whether change is initiated proactively from within or mandated from without, it inevitably creates tension. Being aware of and managing this tension is key to effectively leading and implementing organizational and individual change.

People process change on two levels: on a rational/intellectual level and on an emotional level. You must appeal to and address both. The announcement of a given change will create a mix of reactions – ranging from denial, shock, anger, resistance, fear, and helplessness; to relief, hope, excitement, and revitalization. No matter where people begin in their reactions to change, your goal is to get them to the same endpoint: *committed* to making it happen as effectively as possible. Here are some of the things you can do to make that happen:

- *Make change personal.* No matter how widespread or far-reaching the need for organizational change, making it happen ultimately comes down to individuals. Organizations don't change; people do. People's lives, habits, routines, daily activities, confidence, comfort, and surroundings will be affected. Everyone responds differently. Empathize with the variety of reactions. Listen and respond to those differences rather than projecting your personal response to the change onto others.
- *Involve people early and often.* The roots of commitment, ownership, and implementation are formed by engaging the people affected by the change. We don't argue with, resist or fight our own data. We resist change most when it feels like it is thrust upon us or it catches us by surprise or it makes us feel a loss of control.

- *Clearly define the driving forces for the change.* Help people explore and understand what is happening and why. What will be better? What are the likely outcomes if we don't change? Involve people in the analysis of the influences for the change by using a concept developed by Kurt Lewin called Force Field Analysis. This model states that for any situation in which you desire change, there are two competing forces acting on the status quo. *Driving forces* compel change. *Restraining forces* push back against the status quo, trying to prevent the change from happening. If both sets of forces are of near-equal strength, you will find it difficult to change and innovate, so you have two fundamental options: increase the forces providing impetus for the change, or remove some of the counter forces – the obstacles.

- *Clarify a future state.* Help people see what the situation will look like when the change is achieved. Better yet, build a shared vision of this future state to-

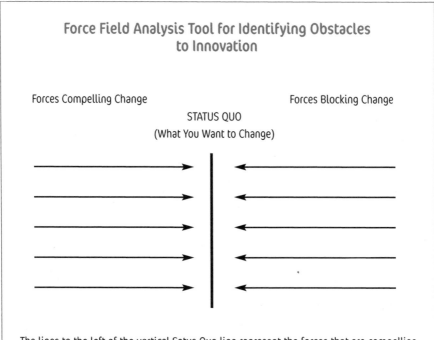

Force Field Analysis Tool for Identifying Obstacles to Innovation

Forces Compelling Change   Forces Blocking Change

STATUS QUO
(What You Want to Change)

The lines to the left of the vertical Satus Quo line represent the forces that are compelling change. Those on the right represent the counter forces that are blocking change. Ask your team to define and describe the two competing forces, and then determine what must be done to increase compelling forces or eliminate blocking forces in order to be able to move the status quo forward toward your goals.

gether. It is much easier to step off the known and comfortable when there is a clear view of the "landing pad."

■ *Take time to process the emotional reactions to change.* Do not minimize or ignore the emotional undercurrents that change creates. Dealing with emotions is a difficult but essential skill for any leader. Unexpressed emotional reactions to change often manifest as resistance, burnout, or passive-aggressive behavior. So take the time to let people discuss and express their fears or concerns. Listen "between the lines" for the emotional components of fear and loss even when people are using purely rational and logical arguments against the change; this may just be their preferred style for dealing with stress, or they may lack awareness of their own feelings. It's also worthwhile to confirm the positive reactions and emotions to ensure expectations align with anticipated outcomes of the change.

■ *Engage resistance.* Don't just assume that the resistance to change is unfounded. As a leader it can be easy to have a knee-jerk reaction to resistance – labeling it a problem. But there may be nuggets of wisdom and insight hidden in the resistance, and you would be well served to listen to and explore them further.

A simple test for change readiness

Just about every facet of life we can think of – the wars searing the globe, the economy, the political landscape, the environment, the social evolution of families and communities, competition – is contributing to a universal pressure to constantly change the way the world does business.

Are you and the people you lead ready? You might be surprised by the response if you put yourselves in a position that really tests your flexibility.

We put one client company in just such a position with a simple exercise. We facilitated the first day of a three-day meeting that included 120 leaders from all over the world, all of whom worked for a global software company. Our job: to help them prepare for change and learn some innovation-mindset skills.

A short time into the session, with these leaders seated eight to a table, we imposed an arbitrary change upon them. Through a random process, we designated four people at each table to move to new spots in the room – under certain conditions. Two people leaving the same table could not sit together at a new table. People arriving at new tables could not sit in empty chairs. The people chosen to move were to take everything they had with them; they weren't coming back. The idea was to invoke change that would leave essentially no one in the room unaffected.

A fair amount of chaotic movement and noise ensued. A few people jokingly sat on each other's laps or on tabletops until they figured out that "not sitting in an empty chair" can mean asking someone already seated to move to a new spot at the same table. Some people were laughing. Others were grousing. After about three minutes, everyone was relocated and mostly resettled but still fidgeting a bit. Some people were smiling. Others looked as if they had sat on something messy.

Once everyone was resettled, we asked for some reactions. A woman seated near us was practically in tears and said, "I'm about ready to leave." We were shocked and inquired why. She had gone to two different tables and been turned away. Her colleagues seated there were unwilling to move as she requested, unwilling to play the silly game.

The irony is that this group had come together for three days to totally overhaul its worldwide service operations. They had, up to that point, been functioning as separate service bureaus in their countries of operation. The new strategy was to realign themselves as "one worldwide virtual team." The three days together were to be a major investment in beginning to implement the new structure. The question we posed in response to this development, and the biggest challenge for those three days, of course, was, "If you were unwilling to change seats in a meeting room, how likely are you to make the dramatic kinds of changes the company is requiring in this reorganization?"

While on the surface the exercise might seem silly, it has a valid and telling purpose. This exercise is a perfect metaphor for real life. Change of this kind happens in the business world every day. It hits without reason or explanation and often falls outside our ability to control it. A gut reaction to an imposed change is instinctive. In the end, it doesn't really matter much whether your first response to being asked to change your seat in a conference room or to reorganize into a worldwide virtual team is positive or negative. What matters most to you in leading innovation is how quickly the people you lead can move themselves back on track to deal with the matter at hand.

To help make that shift as quickly as possible, we remind you again: don't deny the anger or the joy change creates for people. We're all wired differently.

Some people dread any kind of interactive activities in meetings. Some people thrive in jobs that constantly change. There are many experts who counsel about the need to acknowledge the losses, gains, and ensuing emotions any change can trigger.

At some point, however, you have to move forward. If your car has a flat tire, no amount of cursing your bad luck will get you rolling again. If you want to drive, you must simply get out the jack or call a tow truck, get on with changing what needs to be changed, and then move on.

How to uncover obstacles

What's the most powerful force in the universe? Watts Wacker, a futurist, and considered to be among the elite consultants working behind the scenes with some of the world's most prominent companies, once told *Fast Company* magazine, "Lots of people think it is love. Einstein said it was compound interest. I think it's *denial*. It's so easy to get locked into seeing the world from your particular engagement with it."

We agree: denial is a formidable force, especially when it comes to pretending self-inflicted obstacles don't exist. One of the most effective ways to counteract obstacles to innovation is to get aggressive looking for them, but to do it in nonthreatening ways. Here are five proven strategies.

Strategy #1: Put negativity to positive use

Let people complain. In fact, *demand* they complain.

Even if your people aren't troubleshooting your operations, your customers and competitors are, and they will take business away from you in the process. We are not talking about the whining "someone needs to fix this" variety of complaint. If you have created Linkage, your team will be compelled to passionately point out what is not working well and what should be done about it. You need to foster these discussions and help prioritize the obstacles to be addressed first.

- Bring your team together. Describe the challenge you want to address. For example, your goal may be to establish quality customer service as the factor that distinguishes your organization from your competitors. Ask the team to list everything that could possibly go wrong in a typical service encounter with your organization. Instruct them to focus on anything and everything that gets in the way of the average team member being able to provide great service. Make sure the conversation doesn't get personal. Don't let the team blame specific individuals. Stay focused on the tasks.

- Next, pull together the results. If your group is small and time is plentiful, discuss all the ideas and problems. If your team is more than ten people, it might be most effective to first work in small groups. In that case, you may want to have each group categorize and/or prioritize the top five obstacles identified. Determine which have the greatest negative impact on performance and make those your focus for problem solving.
- Don't assume this has to be sober, heavy work. An effective twist on this process is to encourage exaggeration and humor. Use a humorous video clip or personal story about a poor service experience to start the process. If you really want to stir up creativity, ask small groups of people to present three-minute skits or creative presentations highlighting two or three key obstacles.

Your next step, which we'll explore more in Section 4 – Opportunities: Mess with Success, is to come up with creative ways to eliminate or overcome the obstacles identified.

Strategy #2: Schedule sacred dinosaur hunts

"Sacred Dinosaurs" is a concept from *Break-It! Thinking*, a training workshop developed with Louis Patler and The Learning Design Group. Sacred Dinosaurs are systems, processes, habits, mindsets, and routines that are no longer valid or effective but nonetheless remain as unchallenged standard operating procedures. They become sacred when you take them for granted, assume they are valid, and think there is little you can do to change them. As a result, Sacred Dinosaurs become part of your organizational environment. Unquestioned, they burrow into the subconscious, which makes them very difficult to round up, even though they have outlived their usefulness and should become extinct.

The results are counterproductive, painful, and maddening. Pat Townsend, a consultant and author, tells a story from his days in a leadership position inside a major insurance company. It is an experience that typifies the pain outdated performance requirements can cause. Weekly, a new employee spent hours organizing decks of index cards related to claims and customers, and then delivered them dutifully to a worker in another department. After one delivery – the last one, as it turned out – the new employee happened to turn back toward the colleague to whom the completed project had just been delivered, and watched as the cards got dumped into a wastebasket. No one had told the new employee the cards were no longer needed.

Common varieties of unproductive Sacred Dinosaurs are:

Obsolete/Invalid Values and Beliefs: To survive today, corporate culture must be entrepreneurial in nature – fast-moving, innovative, and risk-taking. This means challenging the basic thinking and structure of the corporation and/or industry as a whole, leaving no room for Sacred Dinosaurs to roam.

Archaic Policies and Procedures: Often we get caught in a classic Catch-22 situation – "If it's still around, it must work; and it must work because it's still around." Most corporate and departmental policies and procedures are inherited from predecessors, and often we fail to question their utility or to explore alternatives. You need to question policies and procedures that no longer serve a clear purpose, especially those that may have been unwisely instituted on a wide-scale basis to correct an infrequent or minor problem. A 100 percent policy for a 1 percent problem can cause tremendous waste, work-around, and frustration. Deal with narrow problems in a much more focused and direct manner.

Unproductive Routines and Habits: These Sacred Dinosaurs are most often found on a personal level. They stifle your productivity, creativity, and motivation. We know plenty of managers, for example, who persist in believing that fixing problems themselves is the fastest way to handle shortfalls in the work quality of the people they lead. This is a Sacred Dinosaur for a couple of reasons: it distracts from other leadership responsibilities that only they *can* handle; it also inhibits staff development and shuts down the creativity others might bring to the challenge if guided to make improvements.

Rounding up Sacred Dinosaurs need be no more complicated than inviting people to talk about them. Your biggest challenge may be your ability to create a sense of trust and security. Let people know you are not suggesting all policies must go. You don't want anarchy and chaos any more than you want complete stiltedness. Make it clear no policy or procedure is too sacred to discuss, and that you won't be defensive.

Earl Bakken, co-founder of Medtronic, often made his feelings clear about institutional policies and procedures: The fewer the better. Policies that inhibit flexibility and freedom, Bakken says in *Reflections on Leadership,* inhibit personal and corporate growth. "One of the saddest lines the leaders of a technology company can hear is the complaint, 'We spend 10 percent of our time coming up with new ideas – and 90 percent trying to work those ideas through the system.'" He advocated "stripping away the policy cobwebs that impede innovation, [so] we can afford our creative people the freedom not only to develop fresh ideas, but also to see those ideas through to fruition."

Strategy #3: Don't blame technology

Technology is not innovation, nor is the lack of technology the root of all evil.

We have never worked in an organization where people told us they had all the technology they needed. To the contrary, we often find people inclined to point to the inadequacies in their hardware and software as the biggest obstacle to change and improvement. For example, we asked 180 managers in a large financial services company to list the single biggest obstacle to their ability to provide outstanding customer service. More than one-third flagged technology-related problems. And the ruckus that developed during the discussion on this topic threatened to drown out conversation about any other obstacles.

And that's the problem.

Technological shortfalls can hurt an organization's ability to compete. But leaders who allow themselves or others to use this excuse as a comfortable rationalization for lack of innovation often sell themselves short. It's too simple to point to outdated or inadequate technology in a business and say, "That's why our performance is less than desired. There's nothing we can do until that problem is fixed."

Roger Dow, senior vice president for Marriott Corporation, learned this technology-is-not-the-root-of-all-evil lesson firsthand years ago in a very low-tech way.

Dow had been working with Marriott's technology and service departments to implement a system that would allow staff at the company's many hotels to recognize returning guests during the check-in process. His early inquiries were met with assurances it could be done, but that it would be a lengthy, complicated, and expensive technological hurdle to overcome and implement.

Shortly after one of these disappointing conversations, Dow checked into a Marriott, as any ordinary guest would, not as a visiting Marriott executive. He was startled when the staff person at the registration desk, who had no idea that Dow was a Marriott executive, said, "Welcome back, Mr. Dow. It's good to see you again."

Dow explained who he was and asked how this property had been able to accomplish what the corporation's information technology experts said would be so difficult and costly.

The staff member was almost embarrassed to explain that when Dow arrived at the front door, the bellman greeted him and asked if he had stayed at this hotel before. And depending upon his answer, the bellman would signal the desk attendant. When Dow came to desk, the bellman stood out of Dow's sight and tugged on his ear, which was the signal to the desk staff that Dow was a returning guest.

Clearly, technology is a critical tool in virtually every business operation, large or small – especially when it comes to keeping track of customer data. Although technological inadequacies can be frustrating, even demoralizing, leaders in innovative organizations still find ways to encourage creativity. Challenge people and give them an opportunity to contribute their ideas, and you'll reveal an incredible resource of energy and innovative problem solving.

Strategy #4: Don't blame time

This is another easy out for people when exploring and discussing obstacles. "We don't have enough time" always turns up in the top three responses when we ask teams what stands in the way of improving performance. We are very aware of the time pressures placed on workers today. Everyone is being asked to do more with less. Less time, fewer resources, decreasing support. But we all have the same twenty-four hours in every day. "Not enough time" is too broad and unspecified a problem to tackle. The clock is not the root cause of time problems. More likely, the challenges are inefficiencies, lack of clear priorities, or insufficient skills.

Your leadership challenge is to dig into what lies beneath the time issue. Why does it feel as if we don't have enough time? What is occupying our time? Are we clear about our priorities? Where are the wastes? What could we eliminate? What could be done in more efficient ways? If we had to do everything we are doing today in half the time, how would we do it?

One of the benefits of breaking down the time issue is that it forces you into a discussion of priorities. A frequent challenge we see with leaders is the inabili-

The Q-12 Tool

One of the simplest and most effective tools we've encountered for helping identify Obstacles comes from the Gallup Organization. It's a list of twelve statements, often referred to as the Q12. They come out of research, conducted by Marcus Buckingham and Curt Coffman with more than 100,000 workers in 2,500 companies in twelve industries, for the book, *First Break All the Rules: What the World's Greatest Managers Do Differently*.

The exercise: Pose these statements to the people you lead and ask them to respond with varying degrees of "yes" or "no." The more frequently and strongly you hear "yes," the more likely you are to be leading a top-performing team.

Every time you hear "no," it's a message about a potential obstacle to innovation. If, for example, people don't know what's expected of them at work, they are not likely to perform at the levels you desire. Let them know, as clearly as possible, what is expected. If they lack the materials and equipment they need to do their jobs, get it for them, or work with them to figure out alternative plans.

		Yes ········· No
1.	I know what is expected of me at work.	5 4 3 2 1
2.	I have the materials and equipment I need to do my work right.	5 4 3 2 1
3.	At work, I have the opportunity to do what I do best every day.	5 4 3 2 1
4.	In the last seven days, I have received recognition or praise for doing good work.	5 4 3 2 1
5.	My supervisor, or someone at work, seems to care about me as a person.	5 4 3 2 1
6.	There is someone at work who encourages my development.	5 4 3 2 1
7.	In the last six months, someone at work has talked to me about my progress.	5 4 3 2 1
8.	At work, my opinion seems to count.	5 4 3 2 1
9.	The mission/purpose of my company makes me feel that my job is important.	5 4 3 2 1
10.	My fellow employees are committed to doing quality work.	5 4 3 2 1
11.	I have a best friend at work.	5 4 3 2 1
12.	This last year, I have had opportunities at work to learn and grow.	5 4 3 2 1

ty to clarify and communicate the absolute top priorities. Without this essential skill, "not enough time" will always be an obstacle. We would all love more time. But you know the old adage, "the work will expand to fill the time allotted." Making time to figure out your priorities when you already feel short of it can be tough, but it allows you to eliminate some of the activities and waste that is interfering with accomplishing your most pressing business goals. The goal is not to prioritize your schedule but to schedule your priorities.

Strategy #5: Challenge your assumptions

Assumptions without foundations can be very limiting when it comes to innovation.

A colleague of ours vacationed in Costa Rica and came away with a vivid personal example of what can happen when you are willing to look beyond what you assume to be true.

He was staying in a cabana that was a short walk along a rain-forest path from a main lodge. Among other things, he had arrived expecting to see large numbers of exotic birds, so every day as he walked that trail he searched the trees looking for the birds he could clearly hear in the branches. They seemed to be everywhere, but for three days he never caught sight of any wildlife in the tree-tops.

Finally, on one trip along the path, he caught a glimpse of a monkey, and he realized that's what he had been hearing all week, not birds. Suddenly, having cleared away assumptions that the calls he was hearing were coming from birds, he saw monkeys everywhere. In part, the trip to Costa Rica was intended to provide time for reflection about a career change. Before he left for Costa Rica, he felt he no longer could contribute to his organization in a meaningful way and was on the verge of leaving to start his own company. The experience with the missing birds and the unexpected monkeys, however, encouraged him to also challenge his assumptions about his career situation, and he returned to his old job with a new outlook, ready to make some productive changes.

How to use obstacles to drive innovation

The techniques and tactics for identifying obstacles to innovation are numerous. We've shared some of our favorites; you'll come up with more of your own.

There are, however, essentially only two uses of obstacles that you need to

Personal Change-Readiness Survey

Circle the number for each question that is closest to your personality or belief. After you've circled your answers, go to the Change-Readiness Scoring Chart (opposite) for insights into how you respond in the face of change.

		Less	like	me	More	like	me
		- - -	- -	-	+	++	+++
1.	I prefer the familiar to the unknown	1	2	3	4	5	6
2.	I rarely second-guess myself	1	2	3	4	5	6
3.	I'm unlikely to change plans once they're set	1	2	3	4	5	6
4.	I can't wait for the day to get started	1	2	3	4	5	6
5.	I believe in not getting your hopes up too high	1	2	3	4	5	6
6.	If something's broken, I'll find a way to fix it	1	2	3	4	5	6
7.	I get impatient when there are no clear answers	1	2	3	4	5	6
8.	I'm inclined to establish routines and stay with them	1	2	3	4	5	6
9.	I can make any situation work for me	1	2	3	4	5	6
10.	When something important doesn't work out, it takes me time to adjust	1	2	3	4	5	6
11.	I have a hard time relaxing and doing nothing	1	2	3	4	5	6
12.	If something can go wrong, it will	1	2	3	4	5	6
13.	When I get stuck, I'm inclined to improvise solutions	1	2	3	4	5	6
14.	I get frustrated when I can't get a grip on something	1	2	3	4	5	6
15.	I prefer work that is familiar and within my comfort zone	1	2	3	4	5	6
16.	I can handle anything that comes my way	1	2	3	4	5	6
17.	Once I've made up my mind, I don't easily change it	1	2	3	4	5	6
18.	I push myself to the max	1	2	3	4	5	6
19.	My tendency is to focus on what can go wrong	1	2	3	4	5	6
20.	When people need solutions, they come to me	1	2	3	4	5	6
21.	When an issue is unclear, my impulse is to clarify right away	1	2	3	4	5	6
22.	It pays to stay with the tried and true	1	2	3	4	5	6
23.	I focus on my strengths not my weaknesses	1	2	3	4	5	6
24.	I find it hard to give up on something even if it's not working out	1	2	3	4	5	6
25.	I'm restless and full of energy	1	2	3	4	5	6
26.	Things rarely work out the way you want them to	1	2	3	4	5	6
27.	My strength is to find ways around obstacles	1	2	3	4	5	6
28.	I can't stand to leave things undone	1	2	3	4	5	6
29.	I prefer the main highway to the back road	1	2	3	4	5	6
30.	My faith in my abilities is unshakable	1	2	3	4	5	6
31.	When in Rome, do as the Romans do	1	2	3	4	5	6
32.	I'm a vigorous and passionate person	1	2	3	4	5	6
33.	I'm more likely to see problems than opportunities	1	2	3	4	5	6
34.	I look in unusual places to find solutions	1	2	3	4	5	6
35.	I don't perform well when there are vague expectations and goals	1	2	3	4	5	6

Change-Readiness Scoring Chart

	BELOW 22 POINTS	22-26 POINTS	22-26 26 POINTS
PASSION			
RESOURCEFULNESS			
OPTIMISM			
ADVENTUROUSNESS			
ADAPTABILITY			
CONFIDENCE			
TOLERANCE FOR AMBIGUITY			

PASSION: Add up questions 4, 11, 18, 25, and 32. This is your total score.

RESOURCEFULNESS: Add up questions 6, 13, 20, 27, and 34. This is your total score.

OPTIMISM: Add up questions 5, 12, 19, 26, and 33 – then subtract that subtotal from 35 to get your total score.

ADVENTUROUSNESS: Add up questions 1, 8, 15, 22, and 29 -- then subtract that subtotal from 35 to get your total score.

ADAPTABILITY: Add up questions 3, 10, 17, 24, and 31 – then subtract that subtotal from 35 to get your total score.

CONFIDENCE: Add up questions 2, 9, 16, 23, and 30. This is your total score.

TOLERANCE FOR AMBIGUITY: Add up questions 7, 14, 21, 28, and 35 – then subtract that subtotal from 35 to get your total score.

Check which range you fall into for each characteristic. The optimal range for each is 22 to 26. Every human trait comes with plusses and minuses. Too much passion, for instance, can overcome common sense. Too little can lower a persons' motivation.

The traits measured in this assessment are especially important in dealing with the stressfulness of change. Nobody is perfectly suited to dealing with change. Understanding your own personality relating to change will help you guard against stress.

think about. Once you've identified your obsolete policies and procedures, Sacred Dinosaurs, and faulty assumptions:

1. Use the obstacles to determine what you can do to clear away the most obtrusive barriers. Sometimes all the innovation that is required in a particular situation is to identify the problem and remove it. Our friends at the ice rink have a policy that says, "No skate rental." We suspect it won't take a breakthrough idea to figure out how to say "Yes," instead. They'll need to ask why they say "No," and what can they do to eliminate the counter-productive justification for that response.
2. Use the obstacles to focus your efforts to generate ideas about changes and improvements for your operations. Pick a problem and get creative together to fix it.

Section 4 of *Leading Innovation* focuses on Opportunities. Among other things, in that section, we will give you ideas and tools that will help in eliminating obstacles and for generating ideas for changes and improvements to compensate for conditions limiting your ability to lead innovation.

Overcoming the change obstacle

Change is.

Let that sink in for a minute. The world is a pressure cooker of constant, high-speed, high-tech, high-finance, multicultural, instantaneous global interactivity from which none of us can hide. And that force is guaranteed to increase.

Change isn't good. It isn't bad. It just is…and always will be. It's not something to fear, although when you impose change upon the people you lead – when it's being done to them – fear and resistance are often the natural first reactions. With the right outlook, though, change is opportunity knocking. The challenge is to help people understand change, embrace it, and believe in their ability to work with it to create their own future.

It is important to understand the difference between external change and internal change when it comes to the choices people must make in order to grow. Things are happening "out there" in the world every day that influence our lives and over which we have little or no control. People are born and die. Businesses open and collapse. Technology and biology collide. The earth quakes, rivers flood, and information streams between continents and even planets at the speed of light.

You can help others cope by making sure they learn stress-reducing ways to react to that kind of external change. Help them distinguish between those things they can change and those they can't, and reinforce that it's wasteful to worry about what they can't influence. Set a healthy example by the way you manage internal change in proactive, opportunistic ways.

Fred Smith was a student at Yale University when he observed the changing need for quick delivery of information between businesses around the world. He wrote a paper describing what he saw as a personal opportunity in that change. His professor disagreed and gave him a relatively low grade of C, saying the idea was interesting and well formed but unfeasible. Smith, of course, went on to create Federal Express, the company that forever changed the delivery business.

Chapter 8

Foundations of an Innovative Work Environment

As for the best leaders, the people do not notice their existence. The next best, the people honor and praise. The next, the people fear, and the next the people hate. When the best leader's work is done, the people say, "we did it ourselves!"

—Lao-Tzu

Put good people into a bad system and the bad system will win almost every time.

In the course of our working lives, we've both been employed places where we fought doggedly to change leadership and management practices we believed were counterproductive for our organizations, unhealthy for employees, and detrimental to customers. We saw obstacles that needed to be cleared away and got out our brooms.

In some cases, we were effective in helping create positive change. In other situations, the system was too strong and we didn't have enough influence to change things significantly. We felt frustrated, powerless, and demotivated by the perpetuation of systemic problems.

This phenomenon of getting caught up in the self-perpetuation or self-preservation of a system has long been the focus psychological studies. In 1973, psychologist Phillip Zimbardo conducted an experiment at Stanford University that showed the startling capacity people have for assuming roles defined by an existing system. He created a mock prison in the basement of a psychology lab and assigned student participants in the study to play roles as guards and prisoners. At first, there was mild conflict between the two groups, but it escalated quickly, and the experiment was ended prematurely when the guards began to physically abuse the prisoners to quell their rebelliousness. *Psychology Today* reported that the situation got dangerously out of control. Just six days into the study, students were depressed, crying uncontrollably, and suffering from psychosomatic illnesses.

In *The Fifth Discipline,* Peter Senge points out that we often have the power to alter the systems and structures within which we operate. But, he says, "more often than not, we do not perceive that power. In fact, we usually don't see the structures at play much at all. Rather, *we just find ourselves feeling compelled to act in certain ways.*"

Your challenge in leading innovation is to make sure your management structures and systems – and your leadership style – *support* rather than *sabotage* a culture of change and improvement. A productive first step is to identify the systemic and structural obstacles – whether they are stated policies or unwritten management practices – that are inhibiting performance.

Systemic obstacles

John King, a Six-Sigma certified black belt and a former division president for Textron Financial Corporation, has paid diligent attention to dealing with systemic obstacles and has watched his own organization benefit from these efforts.

"We were always good at generating new ideas and initiatives, but we weren't very good at developing ownership, building support, and acting quickly." So he started looking for ways to improve.

The first obstacle to clear, King says, was senior leadership's practice of taking exclusive ownership for important issues.

"We had to let the managers and supervisors be accountable. Senior leaders needed to break down the political barriers that blocked initiatives, but they also needed to believe we would get better production if we supported and championed ideas rather than always being personally responsible for finishing the endgame."

Trust, King says, was a critical factor in removing this obstacle. And building trust clearly started with King's faith that people would rise to his challenge.

"It's part of human nature and team dynamics that when you involve people, you inspire better and faster outcomes. The biggest trust-building factor for me was *letting go.* I let other people succeed. I let those with ideas and the initiative to push them forward take the lead."

People throughout the company saw King allowing employees – at all levels – to play key roles in big projects. It became clear that things were different under his leadership. "You have to let the people you lead take risks with their ideas; let them determine the outcomes."

As this philosophy and practice cascaded from his position, King says, the leaders who reported to him gradually started saying, "My job has changed. It's no longer always about my hands-on work. I've got to support the team I lead, give them the tools and the time, and get upstream help for them." And then, King says, the benefits started to multiply.

"People saw that they could act on their ideas, and that they'd be given time and resources. They saw it was okay to challenge the status quo… that it was okay to act, even on ideas that turned out to be bad, because the process would help us learn quickly and move on." King says, "Failure is as good as success because they both raise more ideas." And he leads in a way that makes that message clear.

"It's one thing to have an innovative idea; it's another thing altogether to really own what it takes to make that idea a reality. I've seen the number of true 'stakeholders' in our company grow, along with a greater sense of ownership about our business."

That sense of ownership, more than anything else, is what keeps people committed and working for innovation even when they run into problems or are feeling overloaded. As a leader, you can't and won't always be at somebody's side when trouble arises. With the kind of support King describes, people will prevail through even the toughest situations, if they are working for things in which they have a personal stake.

Although King's success in clearing obstacles and fostering innovation at Textron Financial started with his faith in people's ability to grow with the challenge, it wasn't an unqualified confidence, given blindly. King says he watches for indicators that people are ready and able to handle the challenge.

"I look for signs of their commitment to an idea. How much time are they putting in on special projects? How do they handle the barriers they encounter? How effectively and quickly are they moving on key objectives, and how quickly do they respond to problems? How much buy-in do the idea owners create with the rest of the team? A person's idea is like the flame of a candle. If you have one candle burning, you 'see the light.' But how much brighter can you make the light if you surround it with more candles?

"My role as a leader is to help keep the team focused on the final results needed, and to make sure the key stakeholders are clear about the impact the project can have on the customer, the company, and on them personally.

"I ask key stakeholders, 'Why are you doing this? What is it about this project that you really believe in?' I believe people have to be able to express their ideas in terms that provide a clear understanding of those kinds of results."

With this mindset, King says, he finds his leadership role constantly shifting with teams. One project involved making online payment an option for customers. "My role varied. I moved from being in front of the team to being behind. There were lots of small innovative ideas developed as solutions. I focused on the exchange of ownership for those ideas. I made sure people felt the impact of the solutions they offered, the accolades, and the customer comments.

"In addition, I worked on making sure the team was aligned. I delivered important feedback, broke down barriers for them where I could, and worked to make people more visible in the company – letting them handle company updates, for example."

King also makes a practice of spreading responsibility around in a group. "When passing the torch on a project, it is important not to pass one big torch to one individual, but to pass many small torches – to have several people carrying an idea forward. To get full implementation of an idea, it's the people who have to say, 'Let's go!'"

The online payment project was King's, and then it migrated. "But I didn't lose it. The transfer was intentional. My performance is gauged on, and I am personally rewarded for, outcomes." And the outcomes were there.

An added "bonus" for leading this way, King says, is that he gets more opportunities to work with "bad teams" – teams that are broken, dysfunctional, or just unable to make progress on projects everyone agrees are worth pursuing.

Many Six-Sigma practitioners differ with King's leadership approach. They believe *they* must be the doers. "I want to create an environment with many leaders," King says. "Projects move faster. We get better results."

One bad team King inherited had been stubbing its toes for more than four months when he stepped in to help. Under his leadership, the single project became six, all with significant revenue potential attached, and all were up and running effectively in thirty days.

Three tools for razing obstacles

There are many factors in creating an innovation-friendly work environment. Three of the most important have to do with valuing mistakes, protecting people's anonymity when that will help expose issues that may feel too risky to discuss openly initially, and looking at situations from multiple points of view.

Value mistakes

In most work situations, mistakes are not fatal. But the fear of making mistakes can be a debilitating obstacle when it comes to leading innovation.

In part, the problem lies in leaders not having enough faith to take an approach similar to what John King described – not being able to let go of taking personal, hands-on, command-and-control responsibility for important work.

The problem is also exacerbated by the perception that mistakes mean failure. And when that is the case, intimidation usually follows, resulting in a pervasive fear that making a mistake will bring down a severe personal penalty.

The godfather of seeing the value of mistakes, of course, was inventor Thomas Edison, who held nearly two thousand patents, including components for the world's first incandescent light bulb. In the late 1870s, he gathered a team of experimenters and craftsmen and worked around the clock for months trying to discover a bulb filament that would last more than a few seconds before burning out. An observer commented to Edison that his thousands of experiments and hours of work seemed to have been a failure. Edison said, "I have not failed. I've just found ten thousand ways that won't work."

W. Edwards Deming was one of the most influential forces in the Total Quality Management movement. His work helped restore the Japanese economy after World War II, and his success there played a leading role in influencing an overhaul of business practices throughout much of the rest of the world, starting in the late 1980s. In his book, *Out of the Crisis,* Deming laid out fourteen premises for success. Number eight is: Drive out fear, so that everyone may work effectively for the company.

Some high-profile leaders have used differing strategies to make this a reality.

Sergio Zyman was the brand-marketing executive who led Coca Cola into one of the most disastrous product launches of all time, the introduction of New Coke in 1985. He survived in the company for another year, but left "wounded," as *Fortune* magazine described him. "If ever there were a failure destined to kill a career, New Coke was it."

Seven years later, however, the executives at Coke looked anew at Zyman's departure and brought him back at an even higher level of responsibility, as chief of global marketing. When *Fortune* looked into this strange twist of events, Robert Goizueta, who was Coke's CEO at the time, said, "Sergio is a product of a change in our thinking. We became uncompetitive by not being tolerant of mistakes. The moment you let avoiding failure become your motivator, you're down the path of inactivity. You can stumble only if you are moving."

In the end, Goizueta said, "Judge the results. We get paid to produce results. We don't get paid to be right."

The results were outstanding. The beverage maker brought back the old-formula Coke seventy-nine days after the fateful launch of New Coke and saw its biggest ever one-year increase in sales. It reversed the share-price decline it had been experiencing against Pepsi, its top competitor. The recovery was so successful it spawned urban legends that the New Coke flop had been intentional. Not so, but as Goizueta told *Fortune,* "If I could have a New-Coke situation every decade, I would. Absolutely." Yet it apparently took seven years for the company's leaders to realize they had mishandled Zyman's fortuitous blunder.

It's in this kind of environment that makes individual employees willingly and energetically take up the challenge to become self-reliant. In time, they learn to leverage their strengths and begin to take the calculated risks needed to evolve trust, opportunity, and innovation.

Protecting anonymity

Even when trust levels are high, many people are reluctant to share their thoughts about obstacles and problems in their work environment. That kind of silence can be an obstacle in itself, so your job is to find ways to get the issues on the table while minimizing people's sense of personal risk. One way to accomplish this is to find methods to collect anonymous input.

One effective technique is to have people write obstacles on index cards, collect and shuffle them, then randomly discuss the issues one at a time. In a large group, you can have people "shuffle" the obstacles by walking around your meeting room, rapidly and continuously exchanging the cards – without reading them – until you're sure no identities can be connected to the statements. Ask the people to read the card they each hold silently, and then ask for volunteers to read

Thirteen Factors that Foster an Environment of Innovation

Whether you are a CEO, a manager with a smaller sphere of influence, or a champion for innovation with no formal leadership role, there are several environmental factors that are important to monitor as you lead innovation. Each includes questions that can be used to assess how well your work climate fosters innovation.

1. Risk-Taking. Can people take bold action? Is it okay to try new things even when the outcome is unclear? Is individual initiative encouraged and reinforced?
2. Trust and Openness. Do people feel safe in speaking their minds and openly putting forward different points of view? Do you see an inherent trust in people that goes both ways, employees trusting management and the company, and the company trusting employees?
3. Challenge and Involvement. How challenged and emotionally involved do people feel about their work? Do people feel deeply committed to their jobs? Is there opportunity for people to share and act on their ideas?
4. Freedom. How much autonomy do people have in their work? How free are they to decide how to do the specifics of their jobs? How much discretion do they exercise?
5. Playfulness/Humor. Is work a place where it's okay to have fun? Is the atmosphere easygoing, lighthearted, and team-oriented?
6. Open Dialogue. Do people engage in lively discussions about the major issues and challenges? Are diverse perspectives allowed? Is information shared freely with those who need it?
7. Encouragement of New Ideas. Is the atmosphere surrounding new ideas constructive and positive? Are new ideas fostered or regularly shot down prematurely?
8. Resources. Is there access to appropriate resources (information, equipment, time, facilities, funds, etc.) to consider alternatives, test impulses, and try fresh approaches? Is the organization overly bureaucratic?
9. Reinforcement. Is innovation rewarded and recognized? Do managers demonstrate their belief, support, and appreciation for people willing to take risks, speak openly, challenge assumptions and work with passion?
10. Respect. Is there a fundamental respect of each and every contributor within the organization?
11. Opportunity. Does opportunity exist for everyone to excel rather than merely exist? Does the organization encourage people to feel a sense of ownership?
12. Long-Term Perspective. Is it understood that culture is created over time and may take years to change? Is there an appropriate balance between short-term results and long-term viability of the organization and its people, or is everything about next quarter's results?
13. People Advantage. Does the organization view and treat people as the only sustainable competitive advantage? Is training that develops a focus on innovation available to managers and employees?

aloud from cards they think list significant obstacles. Once this conversation begins, you can determine how far to take the discussion. Ask, "Who else has a card
with an obstacle that is similar? Who has something different? By show of hands,
how many of you think the first obstacle is a bigger problem than the second?"

Another simple technique for providing anonymity is to build safety into the
way you phrase your questions about obstacles. If you believe the people you
lead will be hesitant about sharing concerns about obstacles, don't ask directly,
"What do you believe are the biggest obstacles we face?" Instead, ask, "What do
you think our customers, or people in the company, would say are our biggest
obstacles?" This subtle change in the phrasing can initially shift the ownership
for the concern and provide some extra comfort. It's important, however, to
guide the discussion in a way that brings the ownership for solutions back to the
people in your group.

You can also have small groups work together to compare and prioritize
items anonymously listed on index cards or to create lists together of what they
believe others in the organization would consider major performance inhibitors.

With any of the obstacle-fighting tools we offer, it's important not to let the
discussion turn into a gripes-only session. You're identifying the problems so
they can be fixed, not just so people get to vent their feelings. It is helpful to acknowledge the emotions that obstacles can create, but ultimately you must work
on eliminating or overcoming your barriers to innovation and performance.
We'll talk more about that in section 4 – Opportunities: Mess with Success.

As you choose your targets, however, remember the advice in the familiar
prayer: *Grant me the serenity to accept things I can't change, the courage to change
the things I can, and the wisdom to know the difference.*

Looking at alternate points of view

There is always more than one side to every story or situation, but it's often difficult for people to see things from perspectives other than their own – especially when the stakes are high.

One simple technique for helping your team walk in other people's shoes for
a while is to divide your discussion about obstacles into several discussions from
several points of view. We worked with the international audio-visual company
Electrosonic, for example, to help explore a strategy to offer fee-based service
contracts to customers purchasing their high-end electronics equipment. Dur-

ing a strategy session with salespeople, sales managers, technicians, and branch and corporate executives, we asked the team to work in small groups to identify obstacles for each of the key stakeholder groups affected by the change. First we considered obstacles from the point of view of the customers, then the salespeople, then technicians, etc. It is important to address the issues of each stakeholder, one at a time, in order to help people make the mental shift in point of view.

Another exercise for shifting point of view is to role-play. Give your team groups this assignment: You have been hired as outside consultants. You are experts in diagnosing systemic problems in organizations. We need you to tell us everything we are doing wrong (as it relates to the challenge you are addressing). Discuss this in your group and prepare a brief presentation of your key findings, assessments, and conclusions.

A variation on this exercise is to role-play a postmortem discussion. Imagine that your competition has put your organization out of business. What happened? What weaknesses did they exploit? What opportunities did you miss, and what obstacles were to blame?

The last two chapters have focused on Obstacles, but be conscious that all the while you are bringing people together to identify problems, you are also facilitating Linkage. You are involving people in important work, asking for their ideas and opinions, and getting them ready to come up with ideas that will lead to change and innovation. You are helping people see what is in it for them when they take ownership for the organization's problems and their resolutions.

LOOP Leadership is not a linear or step-by-step process. You'll be reminded of that again in section 4 when we focus on Opportunities. You will be learning how to generate ideas for change and improvement, but there will be times when you will find it advantageous to switch over to the process of looking for obstacles. The same will be true when you get to section 5. There, we will help you make plans and commitments for what your team or entire organization needs to do to eliminate obstacles and implement your new ideas.

The costs of misguided management

This following parable isn't exactly Aesop's Fables, but the tale, by an author we have been unable to identify, is a great tool for stirring up conversation about what it takes to create a workplace conducive to change and innovation.

Don't try being a boss like Clarence (you'll see what we mean when you read the story), but consider using this anecdote to help you identify obstacles to innovation. You can take a "negative learning" approach as we described in the "Put Negativity to Positive Use" section in chapter 7: read the story aloud, ask your team first to talk about problematic behaviors and beliefs in your organization similar to Clarence's, and then to discuss what could be done to correct them. Or, read the story aloud, get right into a discussion about what Clarence or Felix could have done differently, and then talk about the lessons that might apply to your team or organization. Here's the story.

Once upon a time, there lived a man named Clarence who had a pet frog named Felix. Clarence lived a modestly comfortable existence on what he earned working at Wal-Mart, but he always dreamed of being rich.

"Felix," he exclaimed one day, "we're going to be rich! I'm going to teach you how to fly." Felix, of course, was terrified at the prospect. "I can't fly. I'm a frog, not a canary!"

Clarence, disappointed at the initial reaction, told Felix, "That negative attitude of yours could be a real problem. I'm sending you to class." So Felix went to a three-day class and learned about problem solving, time management, and effective communication, but nothing about flying.

On the first day of "flying lessons," Clarence could barely control his excitement (and Felix could barely control his bladder). Clarence explained that their apartment building had fifteen floors, and each day Felix would jump out of a window, starting with the first floor and eventually getting to the top.

After each jump, they would analyze how well Felix flew, isolate the most effective flying techniques, and implement the improved process for the next flight. By the time they reached the top floor, Felix would surely be able to fly.

Felix pleaded for his life, but it fell on deaf ears. "He just doesn't understand how important this is," thought Clarence, "but I won't let his nay-saying get in my way." So, with that, Clarence opened the window, threw Felix out, and watched as he landed with a thud.

Next day, poised for his second flying lesson, Felix again begged not to be thrown out of the window. Clarence opened his Pocket Guide to Managing More Effectively and showed Felix the part about how one must always expect resistance when implementing change. And with that, he threw Felix out the window and watched him once again land with a thud.

On the third day, on the third floor, Felix tried a new ploy. He stalled, asking for a delay until better weather would make flying conditions more favorable. But Clarence was ready for him. He produced a timeline, pointed to the third milestone, and asked, "You don't want to fall behind on the schedule, do you?"

From his training, Felix knew that not jumping that day would mean he would have to jump twice the next, so he just said, "OK. Let's go." And out the window he went.

Now, understand, Felix really was trying his best. On the fifth day, he flapped his flippers madly in a vain attempt to fly. On the sixth day, he tied a small red cape around his neck and tried to think Superman thoughts. Try as he might, though, Felix couldn't fly.

By the seventh day, Felix, accepting his fate, no longer begged for mercy. He simply looked at Clarence and asked, "You know you're killing me, don't you?"

Clarence pointed out that Felix's performance so far had been less than exemplary, failing to meet any of the milestone goals Clarence had set for him.

With that, Felix said quietly, "Shut up and open the window," and he leaped out, taking careful aim on the large jagged rock by the corner of the building.

And Felix went to that great lily pad in the sky.

Clarence was extremely upset. His project failed to meet a single goal he set out to accomplish. Felix had not only failed to fly, he didn't even learn how to steer his flight as he fell like a sack of cement. Nor did he improve his productivity when Clarence had told him to "fall smarter, not harder."

The only thing left to do was to analyze the process and determine where it had gone wrong. After much thought, Clarence smiled and said, "Next time, I'm getting a smarter frog!"

OPPORTUNITIES – MESS WITH SUCCESS

Chapter 9

The Power of Mindset

No sense in being pessimistic – it wouldn't work anyway.

—UNKNOWN

> OPPORTUNITIES – The Opportunities phase of LOOP Leadership engages people in generating ideas for improving, changing, and innovating in order to:
> 1. Build upon current successes.
> 2. Create new possibilities for growth and success – personal and organizational.

Opportunities surround us, but what we often see instead are problems, challenges, or obstacles. Because perception is reality, what we see is what we believe, whether it's true or not. And that can be a problem when it comes to innovation. Louis Pasteur said, "In the field of observation, chance favors the prepared mind." Certainly, when you're talking about innovation, "the prepared mind" is defined in large part by knowledge and experience. But a critical second component of an innovative mindset is your ability to inspire yourself and the people you lead *always* to be on the lookout for new possibilities, novel answers, different ways of looking at things, and *always* to be asking penetrating questions and believing there is a better way.

We all see the world through our own filters, which are created from our lifelong accumulation of experiences, knowledge, values, and beliefs. The problem occurs when all of that wisdom turns those filters into blinders, severely limiting or blocking what we see. Consider these vainglorious examples:

- In 1949, *Popular Mechanics* magazine looked at what was happening with the first room-sized computers and boldly predicted, "Computers in the future may weigh no more than 1.5 tons."
- In 1968, a group of engineers at IBM, the company that pioneered the mainframe computer industry, evaluated the first microchips – which would become the heart and soul of personal computers – and asked, "But what are they good for?"
- In 1962, a memo written at Decca records about The Beatles said, "We don't like their sound, and guitar music is on the way out."

Every day, very smart people miss huge opportunities for innovation, due to what they believe to be indisputable truth. Many factors cause people to misread potential, of course, but mindset is critical. Innovation is not a specific process or set of rules to follow, nor does it "arrive" at a goal and stop. It is a way of thinking. Innovation includes:

- The attitude that risk and failure must be tolerated.
- The conviction that change should be actively sought out rather than resisted or tolerated, because growth and opportunity are impossible without it.
- The ability to challenge assumptions and mental models and to shift paradigms when the need arises.
- The habit of asking how to maximize potential rather than minimize losses.
- An understanding of the power of passion, joy, and humor in the creative process.
- A tolerance for ambiguity and uncertainty on the journey to solutions.
- A deep appreciation for how diversity enriches a team's ability to come up with fresh and novel ideas.

Only the past is definite, and sometimes even it defies analysis. Yet it's attractive because at least it's over and won't change much. However, if we orient our present and future activity mainly by looking backward, what evolution or innovation is possible? The desire for security causes us to cling to the comforts of the past and the status quo. Innovation, on the other hand, occurs through the bold embrace of the unknown and uncertain. It's this mindset that can create freedom from the past and the present, and create an exciting future.

Alternate Uses Tool

One of the greatest obstacles to an innovative mindset is the belief that there is only one anything – only one right answer, only one correct way to do things, only one proper use for a particular product or service.

Use this quick, fun, high-energy exercise in a team meeting to help challenge that way of thinking. It is especially effective if you are meeting to conduct a brainstorming session or to do some creative problem solving as a group.

1. Select a common item to show to your group – an umbrella, a child's flotation device, a garden trowel, a stapler. Just about anything will do.
2. Divide your group into teams of roughly equal size.
3. Show the item to the entire group and instruct each team to work together to come up with twenty alternate uses for the item as quickly as possible. In your instructions, emphasize that any idea counts, no matter how silly or impractical it may first sound. Tell the teams to stand up as soon as they have written twenty ideas. When the first group finishes, encourage them to keep adding ideas to their list as they stay standing and waiting for the other teams to finish.
4. When all the groups have listed twenty ideas and are standing, ask for someone on the winning team to read its list aloud. (Get ready to hear the other teams groaning in reaction to the "bad" ideas on the list. Remind the groups that in this exercise there is no such thing as a bad idea.)
5. Ask the groups to sit again and then repeat the process, but this time instruct the groups that they are racing to be the first team to come up with ten more ideas.
6. Debrief the exercise. Ask for observations about the process, how ideas flowed, how people felt expressing their ideas, how round one compared to round two. Look for insights about how some totally crazy and impractical ideas may have led to others with real potential. Then draw out comparisons that relate to how teams typically function in your organization and lessons you could apply toward becoming more innovative.

You'll notice the first time through the brainstorming that some people will get bogged down trying to come up with ideas that would really work. That slows things down. The ideas should flow more freely and quickly when they suspend judgment. And that is what you are after.

You can also use this process to generate creative ideas related to specific business challenges.

Ask your team to unleash their thinking to come up with alternative uses for the products or services your organization provides. Generate as many ideas as possible, and then look for the nuggets of ideas with true potential that you can refine and implement.

Firehosing versus Firestoking

"Firehosing" is a sure way to kill innovation. It's a term from the book *If It Ain't Broke ... Break It!* by Louis Patler and Robert Kriegel. Firehosing is dangerous and demoralizing. It undermines ideas. It grows out of a mindset that prefers comfort and certainty, and demonstrates a strong aversion to anything that may require novel thinking. It snuffs out ideas too early and can stifle creativity entirely.

Typical firehosing works like this: Someone offers an idea and the first phrase out of the firehoser's mouth is "No," or "Yeah, but..." Expert firehoses can interrupt an idea before it has even been fully explained and provide detailed factual rationales, insights about bad-news bottom-line realities, or any number of other explanations why the idea could never work.

Firehosing can feel righteous; after all, the advice usually comes from the experience of hard-learned lessons or from a serious responsibility for being prudent with an organization's time, money, and people resources.

Nevertheless, instead of firehosing, you want to invest in "firestoking" – fanning people's ideas to make them hotter and brighter.

Search for and acknowledge the innovation or uniqueness about a person's ideas. If you try, you can find something worthwhile in just about any idea, and once you've found that nugget, you can continue with a collaborative, creative process. A manager at an aerospace company told us an employee who persisted in trying to convince him they could develop antigravity boots was driving him mad. The worker was convinced he had a plan for shoes that would allow people to suspend themselves off the ground. The manager was concerned the employee might be a bit crazy, and tried to avoid this tough supervisory situation as much as possible. Firestoking, he realized, offered a fresh approach. Instead of ducking this person, he showed interest, asked questions, and acknowledged this worker's intense interest in science and entrepreneurship. That switch helped redirect this energy toward other more productive projects.

Look for ways to build on people's ideas. Say, "Yes, and ..." instead of "Yes, but ..." Expand ideas instead of shrinking them. Involve others. Draw out positive, supportive thoughts and ideas from others involved in the project. Use body language that signals interest, support, and trust.

Don't fake enthusiasm. Find something of genuine interest in people's ideas and be sincere in your support. It can be difficult to encourage ideas if you are dealing with somebody who is extremely off track. But if the person has good intent, these techniques can work.

Management guru Tom Peters once said, "If something new is good, then people will hate it at first. The Post-it took twelve years to catch on. FedEx carried about six packages the first night, which is probably twice as many viewers as CNN had the first night. You should not get high scores the first time out with something new."

Albert Einstein said, "If at first an idea is not absurd, then there is no hope for it."

It's important for you to challenge anything about your leadership style that perpetuates the pervasive – and limiting – belief that there is only one right way to do things. You must create an idea-friendly environment by:

- Consistently suspending judgment on ideas at least long enough for them to be heard completely.
- Willingly accepting that any and all ideas offered have some value.
- Looking first for what's good in ideas rather than what's wrong.
- Building upon ideas to make them better, not tearing them apart to discard.

Today's solutions are tomorrow's problems, so it's also important to keep asking questions and to remain open-minded.

Niels Bohr, the Nobel Prize-winning physicist, was once asked if his parents had done anything unusual in his upbringing to help make him so extraordinarily successful. They had, he said. Every day when he came home from school, instead of asking him how he had done on tests or what his grades were, they wanted to know, "Did you ask any good questions today?"

Creating volunteers, not victims

"Victimitis" is a mindset guaranteed to kill innovation. This is a way of thinking that leaves people believing they have little or no control over what is happening in their lives. They feel passive and reactionary, as if the world were being "done unto them" and there is nothing they can do about it.

It is true that there are forces of change and influence in all of our lives over which we have no control. But victims get stuck there. They feel and act powerless, at best, waiting for the change to pass and for things to go back to normal, which of course never happens.

Author Martin Seligman says in his work about happiness and optimism that victims learn this sense of "helplessness." They do this by getting in the habit of allowing setbacks and adversity to become too personal, too pervasive, and too permanent. They take too much personal responsibility for others' negative behavior. They immediately believe *they* have done something wrong whenever someone else is upset. Victims also allow the adversity to spill over into other areas of their lives. They use an inordinate amount of time to process and move on from the change or adversity; it consumes them.

Volunteers, on the other hand, say, "I can't control those forces, but I can control how I respond to them." These people learn to deal rapidly with change and adversity. They are no less upset or affected by challenges. They do, however, have a remarkable capacity to learn the lessons inherent in mistakes or hardships and then let go. They move on all the wiser, unwilling to allow any given setback to define them.

Nurturing optimism

There are those who believe people are wired differently – and permanently. They believe the optimists will always see the world from their proverbial glass-half-full perspective, that the pessimists will always see it from the half-empty point of view, and the cynics will be forever saying, "What damn glass?"

Our experience tells us mindset is alterable, and the benefits of choosing to live with a positive attitude are worth the effort. Optimism is not just about being happier. Numerous studies show that people who deal optimistically and opportunistically with change and adversity are more productive, motivated, energetic, and focused. They learn better, are more creative, and make better decisions about the risks they take. They are even healthier.

To help the people you lead remain optimistic and to see personal opportunity in change and adversity, help them let go of their "OLD" way of thinking:

1. **O**wn the adversity or change. Put it in perspective. Take an *appropriate* level of responsibility for dealing with change or adversity. Going to either extreme – "It's all my fault" or "There is nothing I can do about it" – is ineffective. Much of what happens around us is not a result of our choices or influence and therefore not a reflection of some flaw in us. On the other hand, we always have the power to control our reactions. Engage people in a discussion about the level of personal responsibility they should take for a given event. Act as a sounding board and guide for identifying the appropriate levels of responsibility.

2. **L**imit the effects of the change or adversity. Some people have much too long a memory when it comes to negative events in their lives. Others allow setbacks in one domain of their lives to spread like cancer into others. With the wrong outlook, adversity can quickly cascade and amplify until it becomes overwhelming or gets totally out of proportion with an actual event. There

always comes a point when it is time to forgive, to move on, to learn and let go. Otherwise, the negativity will continue to fester and do harm. You cannot push people through a change or adversity, but you can lead by example and use dialogue to help others regain perspective.

3. **Do something constructive.** As quickly as possible, mobilize the people you lead to do something productive. Taking steps – any steps – to deal with a change is advantageous. Action is the seed of self-empowerment; it emanates from the belief that "I can do something to make a difference." This perspective, an internal locus of control, is extremely powerful in dealing with change and adversity. It builds upon itself. Small actions lead people to a greater belief in their ability to influence the situation. This builds confidence, resulting in greater action, and the cycle of resilience continues to grow. The opposite spiral is also possible, leaving victims paralyzed. Help people focus on the actions they can take within the sphere of their influence.

Turning gripes into goals

Michael Murray, president of Creative Interchange Consultants in Austin, Texas, taught us a gripes-to-goals technique that can also help. Encourage people to complete the following four statements.

Depending on the dynamics in your team, it can work to openly discuss all four statements, or to keep the first three statements private and to use only the fourth to talk with you or others also concerned or affected by the issue at the center of the complaint.

My frustration is…
My real concern is…
What I'm wishing for is…
Therefore, my goal is… (or, Therefore my goal is to figure out how to…)

Finding the expert within

When Charles Handy, the author of *Beyond Certainty,* first grasped the significance of the discontinuity of change in his life, he felt he had been waylaid and misguided by all his previous education. The main lesson he had learned up to that point, he says, is that the "experts" in the world – the teachers, scientists, religious leaders, etc. – had answers to all questions. His job as a student, if he had a problem or a question, was to find the expert with the answer. That belief, he says, was wrong – and crippling.

"It never occurred to me in that world of certainty," Handy says, "that some problems were new, or that I might come up with my own answers. The world is not an unsolved puzzle waiting for the occasional genius to unlock its secrets. The world ... is an empty space waiting to be filled."

That was a powerful shift in mindset for Handy, and the exact outlook you want to foster in your culture. Once this open-minded and hopeful perspective is firmly established, it's possible to carve a wide path for unleashing the creativity inherent in every individual, team, and organization.

Chapter 10

Innovation Styles and Characteristics

Use what talent you possess: the woods would be very silent if no birds sang except those that sang best.

–Henry Van Dyke

Your team comes to the table with a richly varied compliment of creativity, skills, and natural ways of producing ideas and putting them into practice. One of your key leadership challenges is to understand, appreciate, and cultivate that diversity, and there is a great deal of research and theory that can help.

The benefits of understanding the differences delineated in the styles assessment tools developed by various researchers are numerous. They closely tie into points we made earlier about tapping people's unique talents, playing to individual strengths, and reaping the advantages of combining those gifts. Most important, helping people to understand, respect, and value the differences in each other's styles vastly improves a team's potential to work together creatively and effectively. Imagine the difference between what can be accomplished musically by a choir comprised entirely of sopranos as compared to a chorus with a full range of voices and an appreciation of the notion that not everyone should sing the same.

There are potential shortcomings in giving people thinking-preference and/or innovation-style labels. One concern is that placing people into categories can limit your perspective about what kind of performance to expect of yourself and others. There is also a risk in relying on labels if you fail to take into account that there are no purebreds when it comes to behavior styles. No matter what criteria you choose for describing innovation styles, you are likely to find elements of every descriptor in every person. In fact, most proponents of style-analysis methods emphasize that these tests typically suggest a dominant or preferred style, not a one-and-only way of behaving.

Of the many models and approaches that exist to explain how people differ in their styles of innovation or creativity, we'd like to present a few that we feel will help you whether you lead individuals, teams, or whole organizations in being more innovative. We'll describe them here very briefly, but we recommend you look at the resources we will mention if you want to dig into this more deeply.

Visioning, modifying, exploring, and experimenting

William C. Miller describes four innovation styles in his book, *Flash of Brilliance: Inspiring Creativity Where You Work*. They are visioning, modifying, exploring, and experimenting. To understand your personal "mixture of styles," he suggests ranking the following four approaches to innovation from one to four, with one being your most preferred method for finding solutions and four being your least:

- *Visioning*: Seeking the ideal, long-term solution, imagining the best possible outcome.
- *Modifying*: Improving on what you've already done; applying expert opinions in new ways.
- *Exploring*: Starting with totally new assumptions, using metaphors and analogies for new insights.
- *Experimenting*: Playing with the variables operating in a situation, combining the ideas of many people.

Miller reminds his readers that it's important to keep in mind that each style is "a language of innovation" rather than a type of person. An individual may be comfortable and fluent in a couple of styles.

Those who prefer the *Visioning* style tend to think in terms of ideals and long-term, picture-perfect solutions. Visioning entails dreaming, imagining what it would be like if those dreams came true, and then providing direction, inspiration, and momentum to creative projects.

The *Modifying* style, Miller says, focuses on building on and optimizing things that have already been done. Modifiers prefer to improve on what others have started, and they help bring stability and thoroughness to creative endeavors by helping make sure the full potential of ideas gets developed.

With the *Exploring* style, "you seek to challenge core assumptions and discover new alternatives – you *challenge* and *discover*," Miller says. Explorers challenge assumptions and let things unfold without having specific goals or processes in mind. *Exploring*, he says, can lead to radical breakthroughs.

The *Experimenting* style focuses on combining and testing in order to come up with novel solutions. Experimenters test various combinations of ideas and learn from the results. They are process oriented and systematic in their approach. *Experimenting*, Miller says, is an effective way to expand and troubleshoot new possibilities while also building consensus for possible solutions.

Adaptor or innovator

Michael Kirton, author of *Adaptors and Innovators: Styles of Creativity and Problem Solving*, argues that all people solve problems and are creative. His Kirton Adaption-Innovation (KAI) Inventory describes people's creativity, decision-making, and problem-solving styles on a continuum from *highly adaptive* to *highly innovative*. This continuum is a measurement of the amount of structure, and degree of consensus within that structure, that a person prefers when solving a problem or being creative.

Using Kirton's perspective on innovation styles, you'll see that people with a more adaptive personality prefer to approach problems *within* the current structure of generally recognized theories, practices, procedures, systems, policies, references, norms, perspectives, etc. They operate within the current paradigm of the problem. These people prefer to make small advances and continuous improvements. They like to make incremental innovations.

The more innovative personality, on the other hand, prefers to disconnect problems from the way they are currently viewed or perceived and approach them from completely new paradigms. They prefer doing things entirely differently and finding unexpected, new-to-the-world solutions. They prefer to make monumental innovations.

Asking people to work outside their comfort zones creates personal challenges, Kirton says. Thus, asking strong adaptors to do highly innovative work requires them to use a great deal of energy in coping. The opposite is true if you ask strong innovators to perform a lot of adaptive work. Both "mismatches" lead to stress. Within teams, a lack of appreciation for the different styles can severely inhibit collaboration and cohesion.

An interesting finding in Kirton's research is that groups – teams, departments, and even organizations – tend to develop a consensual KAI score, even when you see a wide range of scores within the group. Regardless of your group's degree of consensus, however, leading innovation requires you to make a deliberate effort to help everyone hear and appreciate the adaptors and innovators that may be on the fringes of a largely consensual group.

Kirton does not suggest that either of these styles is right or wrong or that people are purely innovators or adaptors. We all are a mix of the styles, but our dominant preferences produce predictable behavioral differences. Watch for them, nurture them, and put them to good use. You need people with styles all along the continuum from highly adaptive to highly innovative in order to address the varying challenges, opportunities, and changes that organizations, teams, and individuals face today.

Whole brain theory

Ned Herrmann, the late author of *The Creative Brain* and *The Whole Brain Business Book,* created his whole brain theory by combining Roger Sperry's right brain/left brain theory and Paul MacLean's triune brain theory into a single way of explaining how people process, understand, and utilize information.

Right brain/left brain theory says the right and left sides of the brain's cerebrum (the rational thinking part of the brain) handle information differently. The right side is better at nonverbal, visual/graphic, spatial, abstract, conceptual, and relational thinking. And the left side is more oriented to verbal, logical, rational, linear, and sequential thinking.

The triune brain theory describes the modern brain as actually three brains superimposed on each other as they evolved over time. The oldest, smallest, and deepest part of the brain is often called the *reptilian* brain. It handles bodily functions that happen without our having to think about them – breathing, circulation, digestion, etc. The middle layer of the brain is called the *limbic system.* It is the primary seat of emotion, fight or flight instincts, attention, and affective (emotion-charged) memories. The newest and largest part of the human brain, the *neocortex* (the cerebrum), is responsible for our rational, thinking, higher-cognitive functions.

Herrmann overlapped these theories to create a quadrant model of whole brain thinking, which is a metaphorical way of looking at how we prefer to process, store and retrieve, and make meaning out information. Each of the four areas has a different style and preference for thinking and learning. Most people have a dominant quadrant from which they prefer to think and learn, according to Herrmann. But he stressed that a whole-brained approach is most effective.

In simple terms, you will recognize these styles and preferences among people you lead:

- The organized/administrative style
- The analytical/logical style
- The imaginative/innovative style
- The interpersonal/humanistic style

You can intuitively understand that each style of thinking and learning is especially productive in certain situations, even without knowing Hermann's finely

---

Whole Brain Theory in Action

As a leader, it's best to take all four brain quadrants or styles into consideration when working with your team. Incorporate a variety of methods for communicating, mentoring, and leading when you are running a meeting, conveying a concept, or exploring an idea. For example, using the following tactics in a meeting would address different quadrants and, when done together, contribute to creating a whole-brain experience.

Quadrant or Style	Tactic
Organized/Administrative	Provide an agenda Provide a timeline/history
Analytical/Logical	Provide facts/charts Cite research
Imaginative/Innovative	Show a video Brainstorm/mind-map
Interpersonal/Humanistic	Role-play Tell a powerful story

detailed development of these concepts. What's most important to understanding and putting Herrmann's model to work as a leader of innovation is your ability to apply these concepts to individual and group learning and thinking. He believed that individuals and groups can maximize their creative potential by tapping into, utilizing, and developing all four brain quadrants.

Diffusion of innovation

Everett M. Rogers describes five innovation styles in his seminal book, *Diffusion of Innovations*. His work focuses primarily on how people respond to innovation, in particular to the introduction of new technologies. He refers to these styles as "adopter categories," but the insights are also valuable for self-assessment of innovation style.

Innovators are venturesome, almost to the point of obsession, Rogers says. They are eager to try new ideas – often hazardous, rash, daring, or risky ones. They are able to cope with a high degree of uncertainty and are willing to absorb setbacks. Innovators play an important role in helping launch new ideas and products into social systems and markets. Fewer than three people out of one hundred fall into this category, according to Rogers, but their willingness to be the first to accept new ideas is influential.

Early adopters represent approximately 14 percent of the population, Rogers says. In a word, they are respected. They are role models for their more reluctant peers, not too far ahead of the pack and ever mindful that their judgment of new ideas must be judicious and discerning, if they are to maintain their positions of respect. Early adapters decrease uncertainty and speed the adoption of innovative ideas.

Rogers also describes those in the *early majority*. Approximately one in three people fall in this group. They are notable for being purposeful in their innovativeness. "The early majority may deliberate for some time before completely adopting a new idea. Their innovation-decision period is relatively longer than that of the innovator and the early adopter. 'Be not first by which the new is tried, /Nor the last to lay the old to the side' [a quote from Alexander Pope] might be the early majority's motto. They follow with deliberate willingness in adopting innovations, but seldom lead."

The *late majority*, which also makes up about one-third of the population, approach innovations skeptically and cautiously, Rogers says. "The late majority

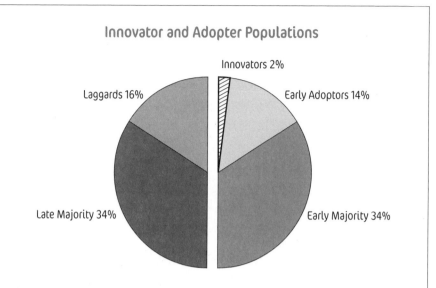

Innovator and Adopter Populations

Innovators 2%

Laggards 16%

Early Adoptors 14%

Late Majority 34%

Early Majority 34%

The people you lead respond differently to innovation. Everett M. Rogers' research suggests that 50 per cent of the people you lead (the Late Majority and the Laggards) will need more time to adjust to and embrace anything new, whether it's technology, a process, or a policy.

do not adopt [innovations] until most others in the social system have done so." It is not the value of an idea that causes the late majority to adopt an idea, but peer pressure. Almost all uncertainty must be gone, Rogers says, before people in the late majority feel safe in adopting an innovation.

Laggards make up the final 16 percent of the population. They are, Rogers says, the last in any social system to adopt an innovation. Laggards look to the past and rely on precedence in all decision making. They tend to be suspicious of innovation, and if they do adopt a new idea, it will often be just after that idea is superceded by another.

Although laggards tend to slow the innovation-decision process in groups, it's wrong, Rogers says, to blame them alone for slow overall acceptance of the new. There may be other factors at work in the system.

Mix and match styles for greatest innovation impact

As you have probably noticed, there are similarities and differences in the four innovation style guides we've described. None of them is perfect. All of them can be useful, if you use them to remind yourself that each and every one of the peo-

Innovation Style
Assessment Tool

One of our simplest and least expensive techniques for identifying innovation styles involves a pile of old shoes and candid conversation.

The exercise works best with groups (or subgroups) of six to nine people. There's nothing scientific about it, but for identifying innovation styles and discussing styles preferences, it's remarkably effective.

Before the meeting, we collect a wide selection of footwear – everything from roller blades to fishing waders. We create a simple tabletop arrangement, randomly mixing in athletic shoes, women's high heels, men's dress shoes, children's tap dance shoes, cowboy boots, fuzzy bunny slippers, and whatever else we have available. The more samples, and the greater variety we have, the better.

We ask each person to identify the one shoe that best represents their personal innovation style. Some people want to pick up the shoes and take them to their tables. But if you have several groups, it's best leave the shoes in the display so others can select the same shoe if they want.

Give each person a minute or two explain their choice to their group. You can deepen the conversation by also asking people to elaborate:

· When is a particular style an asset, when is it a liability, and why?
· What do they appreciate about their styles?
· What do they wish they could change, and why?

With larger groups, we then take five to ten minutes to have subgroups share some of their observations with the whole group. We encourage a general discussion about what the differences in styles mean regarding the ability of the group to work together innovatively.

A variation of this exercise for teams whose members know each other well is to ask people to also select the shoes they believe best represent the styles of the other team members. This conversation can take more time, but it can uncover powerful insights about how people perceive each other and how their styles inhibit or compliment each other.

In one situation, for example, we used this exercise as the foundation of a daylong strategic planning process with the leadership team of a small advertising agency. The process probably would have floundered without the revelations and contrasts the group experienced comparing shoes.

Some folks find it tough to think metaphorically like this, but with a little encouragement and an explanation that we are trying to get people to think differently, this activity has always gone well for us. Simply having a display of shoes on a table when people walk into the room begins the process of shaking up the way people think.

ple you lead comes to you with a unique innovation style.

Your awareness, appreciation, and respect for this diversity will make you a better leader of innovation. You need to develop an eye for and bring out the best in each of your contributors – however you identify their styles – by understanding their individual gifts and unique creative potential. And then, like the conductor of a choir with a full range of beautiful voices, you can maximize the group's performance by helping them complement and support each other's contributions – helping them understand that the power to innovate comes in large part from their differences.

Chapter 11
Creativity Tools

Don't play what's there, play what's not there.

— Miles Davis

Getting creative doesn't have to be complicated. In fact, simplicity is the domain of creativity. Being creative starts with the fundamental belief in your own talents and skills, and it ends with using those unique gifts to see the world a bit differently and to think about things in new ways.

There are thousands of books written about creativity and millions of resources available on the Internet. Nobody can master it all. However, based on our years of reading and research on the subject and our experience and experimentation with real people in real organizations, we have come up with some concepts and tools to help keep things simple but productive.

Improv thinking

If you've ever watched either the American or British versions of the television program *Whose Line Is It Anyway?*, or if you have attended theater performances at places like Second City in Chicago or Boom Chicago in Amsterdam, you have witnessed firsthand the creative genius of improvisational acting. You have seen performers walk onto a vacant stage, with no script or props, and using only a couple of minor suggestions about a location or a situation from the audience, create instant theater. The basic rules of what we have come to call Improv Thinking are as applicable in the workplace as they are in these performance venues. They are as simple as ABC:

Accept the idea being offered. In an improv theater scene, the first performer onto the stage mimes digging a hole in the ground with a shovel. When a second actor enters the scene, his or her first step in the creative process is to *accept* the idea the first performer offers about digging a hole. The scene will work, for example, if the second performer begins digging alongside the first. The scene most certainly won't work, however, if the second performer attempts to alter the scene by ignoring the digging. The lesson: *Not every idea is a good one, but every idea deserves to be heard. You will encourage far more creativity and risk taking if your first instinct with the people you lead is to find something of value in the ideas they offer.*

B*uild on the idea being offered.* In this improv scene, it's not particularly creative to let a fellow performer go on digging alone. Nor would it be very interesting for the audience if the only thing the second performer did was to jump in the hole and also dig. That would quickly get boring. Creativity happens when the second performer does something to move the idea forward, acting, for example, as if he's struck a buried treasure. The lesson: *You will encourage creativity if you find something of value in every idea, and then build on that nugget. Others will catch on quickly to the process and bring new, unexpected ideas and solutions into the conversation.*

C*ommunicate,* **C***ollaborate,* and **C***ooperate.* Part of the magic of improvisational performance is what happens when one performer's ideas about a scene lead it in a direction none of the other performers – or the audience – had thought about or expected. For that kind of creativity to happen, however, all the parties have to be "present," listening carefully, giving feedback, reacting to the changing situation, working together, sharing the spotlight, and trusting and supporting one another – all essential attributes for teams to create and innovate together effectively. The lesson: *You can set the stage for innovative thinking in your team by making it clear to those you lead you are willing to hear their ideas and to work together to fine-tune those ideas for implementation.*

The rules of Improv Thinking are simple to comprehend but more difficult to apply, of course.

John Sweeney is the owner and executive producer of Brave New Workshop, a satirical comedy theater company in Minneapolis that has used the principles of improvisation to create more than 500 productions since 1958. He is also the lead author of *Innovation at the Speed of Laughter: 8 Secrets to World Class Idea Generation.*

In creating new shows, Sweeney says the actors, writers, and producers begin the creative process as a team. They select a random word or phrase of inspira-

Four Tools for Putting More Lightning in Your Brainstorms

- Speed Write. Ask people to write down as many ideas related to your challenge or opportunity as they can in a specified amount of time – five minutes works well. Then compare, discuss, and build on what people have written. Individual writing eliminates "group-think" and other influences from the more expressive or dominant personalities in the group.
- Team Brainstorm. Ask small groups to jointly create a list of twenty ideas as fast as they can. Make it a competition by providing small prizes to the team that finishes first. Have the small groups exchange these lists and then conduct another round of brainstorming to add new ideas not on either list. Adding speed and competition to brainstorming helps the group naturally suspend judgments and censorship of ideas.
- Timed Team Brainstorm. Give small groups a specified amount of time to generate as many ideas as possible related to your challenge or opportunity. Consider using this as a follow-up or a second round to a regular team brainstorm.
- Deep Dig. When you reach the point in brainstorming where the energy seems to have ebbed, take a break, and then come back for one more round of idea generation. Add an outside stimulus to help the group see the challenge or opportunity from another perspective. For example, while they are on break, ask people to find one inanimate object that has traits or characteristics similar to the current challenge or opportunity. When the group reconvenes, have each person explain how their item relates to the challenge. (Also see Lateral Thinking, on page 115.) Briefly review some of the ideas already generated, then challenge the group to come up with ten or fifteen new ideas. Second or third rounds of brainstorming on the same topic are usually tougher, but this is when some of the best ideas will surface, so stick with it.

tion and then work together to generate *600* random, one-sentence statements. Anything goes. All judgment about ideas is deferred until later in the process.

The next step in Brave New Workshop's creative process is to randomly combine pairs of the ideas and see what happens. For one production, they combined the statement "I hate *River Dance*" (the Irish musical and dance production) with "The worst job in the world is being a copier repairman." The result, Sweeney says, was a skit that was a *River Dance* parody about a third-generation copier repairmen. The show earned standing ovations from audiences at intermission – a very rare occurrence.

Opening night of each new production at Brave New Workshop includes approximately twenty-five skits. They are woven together around a thematic title that emerges from the original 600 random statements. Members of the team select the ideas they are passionate about and work together to take them to the next level, with everything evolving through the interaction of the team members. "Once the ideas are accepted," Sweeney says, "they just take off."

When you are leading your team in any kind of brainstorming process, this is the mindset you want influencing your interactions. Share the ABCs regularly. Post notes in strategic locations in your office space. Add them to a tagline in your e-mails. And remind people to use them before you start any discussion in which you are looking for innovative ideas. Also remind people not to judge or evaluate ideas during the idea-gathering stage of a brainstorming session, which is tough to do. You want ideas to flow freely. You can sift through them and weigh their value in a later stage.

Improv practice activities

If you want to develop Improv Thinking with your team on a practice topic before getting into brainstorming on a real challenge, try these two ideas:

1. Ooh baby! What a really bad idea

Set up small groups. Ask each group to come up with a really "bad" idea to discuss at their table. Don't let them spend much time worrying about finding the right bad idea. Anything will do. For example: Our company shouldn't give any more pay raises; we should slam down the phone on any customers that make us angry; or the mayor of our city should issue skateboards to all senior citizens. Next, ask the team to brainstorm ways for making the really bad idea into something that might work. Remind people to Accept the idea, Build on it in some way to make it better, and continue to Communicate and Collaborate in ways that lead to the development of what might actually be a really good or applicable idea. You can complete this activity in five to ten minutes. Ask each team to share its original bad idea and some of the ideas discussed about how to make it better. Then spend a few minutes with your team making observations about the process and the implications if you were to apply this way of thinking and behaving toward real problems. Once people have experienced the energy and positive outcomes that can result from applying Improv Thinking to even a bad idea, they will quickly see the benefits of applying it to your brainstorming efforts and strategic discussions.

2. One-word story

Select five to ten volunteers for this exercise. Ask them to stand side by side at the front of the room. Instruct them that their challenge will be to tell a story together, one word at a time, in sequence from one end of the line to the other. Ask the audience to suggest a title for a story that has never been told before, or suggest a title yourself. Again, just about anything will work: *The Day Goldilocks Met the Three Little Pigs*, *Freddy Went Fishing*, or *The Customer Who Broke the Camel's Back*. Remind the volunteers that there is no wrong way to tell this story – after all, it has never been told before. Ask one person in the line to begin the story by offering one word, and then continue down the line of volunteers in sequence, with each person adding one word, until you reach a logical stopping point. It might take a couple of passes through the line, but in most cases the group will bring a story to closure.

Even in the instances when the thread of the story seems to fall apart, people will have fun with the process and recognize the dynamics of Improv Thinking at work. Most groups will improve if you give them a second or third opportunity.

Spend a few minutes sharing insights about the process and how the learning can be applied to the business challenge at hand. Part of what you will hear is how important it is to listen actively to what others say, how often people feel the urge to control what others think and say, and how important – and how tough – it is to be willing to go with the flow of others' ideas. It is tough to be "present" to the changing story as it makes its way down the line.

Izzy Gesell, the author of *Playing Along: 37 Group Learning Activities Borrowed From Improvisational Theater* explains that, "Contrary to popular belief, improv is not about thinking quickly, being funny, or acting without rules. It is essentially the manifestation of paradox. It teaches there is no freedom without structure, you become spontaneous by practicing spontaneity, and you can feel in control of a situation by giving up control of that situation."

One of the most important lessons about Improv Thinking is learning to appreciate the influence and value of change as it relates to creativity and innovation. Sweeney says, "Improvisers do not try to manage change; they do not try to accept change; they *need* change. It is the fuel of the art form. For the improviser, change leads to the next action step within the scene, and ultimately to the resolution of the scene. With this understanding, it becomes clear that change is a completely necessary part of the solution process. When approaching change in this light, we can become comfortable not only looking for change, but modifying our behavior and environment in a way that will safely and consistently create change."

Lateral Thinking

"Lateral Thinking" is a phrase coined by Edward de Bono, the author of *Six Thinking Hats* and numerous other texts and training products related to creativity. In essence, the art of Lateral Thinking is the ability to let your mind jump off track – or out of ruts – so that you end up in unexpected places with your thoughts and ideas.

The human mind takes creative lateral jaunts all the time, but most of us are conditioned to suppress those "distractions" when problem solving in order to stay focused on the problem at hand. Focus, however, is sometimes a major obstacle to innovation. We become so intent on moving as straight as possible from point A to point C by way of point B that we never see the creative alternative that may lie just off that path.

Humor provides a perfect illustration of Lateral Thinking at work. A joke, for example, often begins with a straightforward, easy-to-recognize situation. The laughs happen, however, when the joke teller jumps the track and takes the listener someplace other than the logical endpoint. Think about a funny story you've heard recently. If you notice where the tale turned toward the unexpected you'll see what we mean. Or consider this story, which finds humor in the simple act of a child looking at an elevator.

A ten-year-old boy came to the big city with his parents for the first time and was extremely excited and awestruck by all the things he was seeing. He had never seen a skyscraper, never stayed in a hotel. In fact, neither had his parents. His rural and isolated hometown didn't even have a single traffic light, and their family never had a reason to venture more than a few miles from their home.

Inside the hotel lobby, the boy was immediately attracted to a wide set of heavy metal doors that had a set of lighted numbers on the wall just above them. He pulled his father by the sleeve to the doors and watched as they suddenly slid apart and a gray-haired man and woman stepped inside. The doors slid closed behind them, and the father and son watched as the numbers above the doors blinked on and off in sequence – 1, 2, 3, 4, 5 – stopped, and then blinked on and off in reverse – 5, 4, 3, 2, 1. Suddenly the doors opened again and out walked a stunningly beautiful young woman holding the arm of a handsome dark-haired man.

At first the boy could hardly speak, but after a few seconds asked, "Dad, what is that thing?"

The father said, "I don't know, son, but go get your mother. We're going in there."

The setup of a joke gets your mind traveling down a known and familiar path. The punch line is funny because it throws your thinking off of this path and gets you to look back at what you were thinking and where your mind was going from an entirely different perspective.

Again, this is the mindset you want dominating your team's thinking, so it's vitally important to develop Lateral Thinking skills. You want to encourage people to share tangential thoughts; some will be off track, and you will want to move on, but others will put you on a new track you will want to follow. And even the off-track suggestions might shake out other thoughts and ideas that otherwise might not have surfaced.

No doubt you have been in discussions where someone made a wisecrack or joking comment that led to a serious and valuable insight because it helped move someone onto a new train of thought. There is a fine line between a group discussion that uses this kind of energy to fuel creativity and those that let it become a total distraction, but the benefits of Lateral Thinking – the fun, energy, and creativity – far outweigh the risks.

Thinking Like Your Innovation Heroes

The next time you are stuck for ideas, make a list of people you admire or of comic book action heroes, cartoon characters, or historical figures. Think about the challenge you face, pick a name off the list and plug it in to the blank in this question: What would [your hero's name here!] do? Asking your team to look at a problem from the perspective of Mickey Mouse or Julius Caesar can be a quick technique for shifting thinking to a new path.

Lateral Thinking exercises

One of our favorite methods for inspiring Lateral Thinking is to ask groups to combine unrelated ideas and concepts.

For example, working with small groups, we ask someone in each group to point randomly to three different items on our Lateral Enterprise List (see page 118). We then ask each small group to work together to combine the three items to create a hypothetical product or service they could market. We give them ten to fifteen minutes to work up a new product introduction for their new offering, then present it to the whole group, using flip charts, markers, and whatever other props or techniques they can conjure. They must name and describe the product or service, define its unique selling propositions and target audience, create a slogan, a marketing campaign, a Web site, etc.

This exercise is extremely effective in helping people to drop their inhibitions and to overcome any natural tendencies they might have for being practical and realistic to the point where they can't be creative. It's tough to be overly serious when you are challenged to create a product that combines dentistry, funeral services, and ostrich farms.

Your challenge is to help people use the same outlook and mindset when dealing with real challenges. There will be a time to get serious, but when you are challenging people to apply Lateral Thinking in search of innovation, it's important to get them into a frame of mind that allows for the same kind of creativity you will see in this Lateral Enterprise exercise.

Once people are loosened up, you can then create your own Lateral Enterprise List as a tool for brainstorming new product or services ideas for your company.

Create a list of your current products and services. Create another list of products or service features offered by other companies you admire (see page 119 for starters).

Select one of your products or services and try randomly combining it with one or two of the features offered by other companies. Don't get locked into a narrow-minded translation of the feature, but do look for ways that feature might stretch or redirect your thinking. It may, for example, be untenable for your organization to offer twenty-four-hour service, but by focusing on extending your customer support services, you may develop ideas that could be beneficial.

Lateral Enterprise Exercise

Pick three enterprises to start your Lateral Thinking exercise (see page 117).

Medical Equipment	Comic Books	Retirement
Dentists	Restaurants	Stump Removal
Telecommunications	Veterinarians	Consultants
Roofing	Mailing Equipment	Gas Companies
Attorneys	Concrete	Bottled Water
Child Care	Employment Services	House Cleaning
Mail Boxes	Pumps	Electricians
Pet Supplies	Golf Courses	Clothes
Carpet Cleaners	Cooking Utensils	Yoga Instruction
Aquariums	Home Health Service	Psychotherapists
Rentals	Snow-Removal Equipment	Modeling Schools
Vending	Tree Service	Optical Goods
Locks	Furnaces	Motorcycles
Radio Stations	Insurance	Stoves
Burglar Alarms	Acupuncturists	Paint
Lighting Fixtures	Internet	Gutters
Sprinklers	Outboard Motors	Beauty Salon
Financing	Playground Equipment	Entertainers
Waterproof Materials	Sheepskin	Schools
Travel Agencies	Autos	Musical Instruments
Real Estate	Glass	Cruises
Florists	Jewelry	Magicians
Landscape Equipment	Trophies	Tattoos
Youth Organizations	Crafts	Holistic Practitioners
Batteries	Environment	Art Supplies
Closet Accessories	Farm	Pizza Delivery
Hypnotists	Investigators	Windows
Sporting Goods	Translators	Ostrich Farms
Aircraft	Sewer	Garbage Collection
Doors	Mortgages	Casinos
Physicians	Catering	Photography
Scuba Diving	Gift Baskets	Tires
Party Supplies	Horse Breeders	Electric Tools
Landfills	Movers	Communications
Fencing	Coffee	Radiators

Lateral Enterprise Product and Service Features List

Create a list such as this – using product and service features offered by companies you admire – to match with a list of products and services your organization offers to create a custom Lateral Enterprise tool. It will help you generate new ideas about how to change or improve your offerings.

Satisfaction Guaranteed ■ 24-Hour Service ■ Mass Customization ■ Total Solutions ■ Made to Order ■ Delivery ■ ISO Certification ■ Lifetime Warranty ■ Technical Assistance ■ One-Day Service ■ Just-in-Time Production ■ Catalogues ■ World Wide Web ■ Paperless Transactions ■ After-Market Products ■ Low-Price Guarantee ■ Double Coupons ■ Frequent Buyer Programs ■ Personalized Service ■ Client-Relations Specialist ■ Centralized Service ■ Trouble Shooters ■ Collaboration ■ Money-Back Guarantee ■ Telemarketing ■ Consultative Selling ■ World Class ■ Technology ■ Qualified Leads ■ Free ■ Add-On Sales ■ Upgrades ■ Online Support ■ Project Management ■ Design ■ Communications ■ Training ■ Customer Recognition ■ Relationships ■ Call Centers ■ Listening ■ Value ■ Help ■ Maintain ■ Prevention ■ Answers ■ Membership ■ Help Desk ■ Free Freight ■ Co-Op Advertising ■ Localization ■

The Five-Hows Solutions Tool

Remember when you were a child and you used to drive your parents crazy by constantly asking the question, "Why?" Well, one of the most powerful things you can do in leading innovation is to restore and encourage that curiosity and persistence in the people you lead, but to switch the question to "How?"

One of the problems with brainstorming is that often the initial ideas generated are not specific enough to implement. For instance, we work with clients who, whether dealing with customer-service issues, strategic planning, or anything in between, often come up with the idea to "improve communication" as a way to change and improve. There's no doubt that improving communication would help, but without a more specific solution, no one knows what to do differently from what they have always done.

So, when we hear a sweeping suggestion such as "improve communication," we guide people to ask the question, "How?" And when they come up with the next suggestion we ask them again "How?" We encourage teams to ask "How?" five times, or until they can look at their solutions and know exactly who will take what action steps and when to begin to implement the ideas.

We use a type of mind-mapping technique for capturing the ideas that peo-

A Five-Hows Mind Map

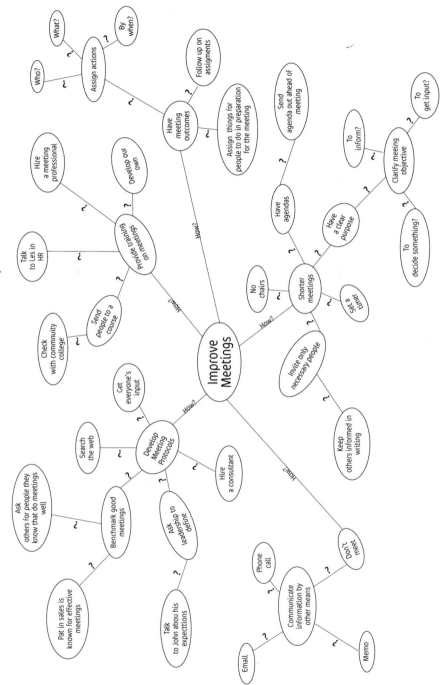

ple generate, using the Five-Hows Tool, because it encourages a free flow of ideas (see page 120).

Begin by writing an idea in the center of a blank sheet of paper. Then ask, "How can I/we do that?" Write the idea in an open area on the page, and draw a line between the two connected thoughts. About this new idea, ask "How?" and write your ideas near it. Draw lines, use circles, different colors of ink, or anything else that helps you organize your thinking. When you have come up with as many specific actionable steps as you can for that idea, return to the original idea and ask "How else can we do this?" Repeat this mind-mapping technique until you have come up with a satisfactory set of ideas that can be implemented.

You will notice that some groups prefer a more linear way of using the Five-Hows Tool. They will do more of an outline of possible ideas, and that's okay. The process can work very well by merely creating a written list of action ideas. The key is to dig deeper by continuing to ask "How?" until you can look at the ideas and say "We know exactly what we have to do next."

As you apply any of these creativity tools, keep in mind that innovation comes in all shapes and sizes. Using Improv Thinking and Lateral Thinking, your two main objectives are to help people instinctively accept and build on each others' ideas instead of automatically shooting them down, and to encourage people to let their minds wander to new places. If you accomplish these two goals, you will see breakthroughs in innovation – big and small.

Chapter 12

The Culture and Strategy of Innovation

We have a strategic plan. It's called doing things.

—HERB KELLEHER, SOUTHWEST AIRLINES

Plans – The Plans phase of LOOP Leadership results in prioritizations, decisions, actions, and personal commitments for what must be done to achieve your desired business results. In this stage, you will:

1. Build commitments, accountability, and reinforcement strategies and tactics into a process focused on sustainable results.
2. Determine who will do what, and by when, in order to move in the direction of your business and innovation objectives.

Plans related to innovation require committing and doing, not talking. You can manage everything correctly in the Linkage, Obstacles, and Opportunities stages of LOOP Leadership, and yet nothing will change unless you create the environment and expectations conducive to taking action. We asked the leadership team at Allianz Life to wrap up a workshop on LOOP Leadership by making summary presentations about which piece of the model was most important. The team that argued for Plans put it this way: Without the P – and the commitments to follow through on ideas for change and improvement – leaders are left in the loo. British potty humor aside, the point is right on.

There are no step-by-step prescriptions for implementing an innovation plan. There are no magic wands. No perfect models to copy. The degree to which you look outside of yourself or your organization for "the" answers to replicate on the innovation journey is the degree to which you may be misunderstanding another important truth about innovation: specific strategies for successfully developing cultures of innovation in organizations are as numerous and unique as the organizations creating them. You will not be able to borrow complete action plans from anyone else.

There are fundamental guidelines, however, that can help you and the people you lead operate with open minds, stimulate and harness your collective intelligence, prioritize the use of resources, direct daily activities, align gifts and talents in new ways, and lock down commitments for getting the hard work of innovation done.

In the next chapter, we will explore tools for prioritizing, deciding, and acting on ideas. But first, we want to highlight a few key elements that directly affect the environment and culture necessary to support the kind of action required by innovation. Whether you are leading an entire organization, a division, or a team of two, the following seven strategies will directly affect the successful execution of your innovation plans. These strategies create a framework for aligning cultural influences, management systems, and people to make your organization more innovative. Depending on the scope of your leadership positions, not all elements of these strategies may be within your control. Focus most of your energies on those that are. As you'll see, although we are officially discussing the Plans stage of the LOOP Leadership Model, implementation of these seven strategies will challenge you to readdress issues related to Linkage, Obstacles, and Opportunities.

Seven strategies for implementing innovation

1. Keep innovation focused on the business issue

Leading innovation isn't really about innovation; it's about business results. As we emphasized in the Linkage phase, it is critical to focus first on your desired business outcomes when you make any effort to drive innovation in your organization. Innovation for innovation's sake is misguided. As you make plans to achieve important business goals, it will become evident that innovation is a tool to take you there, not the end in itself. Whether your goals are to grow, improve service or quality, fix a critical problem, or diversify, it will be clear to those engaged in the process that you need to change and make improvements to reach those objectives, which is simply another way of saying you need to innovate.

In fact, we almost always advise clients against launching innovation initiatives with hoopla and big kickoff celebrations. We find it much more effective to implement LOOP Leadership practices without ever pronouncing the effort as part of some master plan. When innovation starts to happen, acknowledge and recognize that success, but tie the rewards and celebrations to the underlying business objectives. Innovation must be a way of doing business.

2. Secure as much support and involvement from senior leadership as possible

There's a story told about W. Edwards Deming that taught one executive a tough don't-you-get-it? leadership lesson about what it takes to turn ideas into action.

The late total-quality guru was brought in to speak to an auditorium overflowing with employees and middle managers in a company that was gearing up to implement a new strategic business plan. The CEO introduced the esteemed speaker and then, as Deming was beginning his presentation, the leader headed down the side aisle of the auditorium and opened the rear door. Before he could exit, Deming called to him from the podium, asking the CEO where he was going. The CEO, startled but composed, told Deming he had some other important matters to attend to. Deming told the CEO if it wasn't important enough for the CEO to be in this meeting, it wasn't important enough for him either. And Deming left.

Deming's disappearing CEO is a perfect example of a leader convinced it's possible to fulfill a plan by proclamation. It's not. This leader had said all the right things, hired a high-profile expert, and conscripted the volunteers, but his actions provided an unmistakable message that actually implementing all those great ideas would be the job of the "underlings." You don't need a PhD in industrial psychology to predict what kinds of half-hearted actions and plans the general workforce in that organization would be likely to implement.

3. Commit to a long-term innovation strategy

Innovation is not a fad or one-time event. If you think you can do innovation for a year and then move on to your next latest-greatest initiative, you are destined to fall short of your hopes and expectations.

To make sure this kind of endeavor doesn't become a management fad of the month, you must remain consistently supportive of these core competencies and patiently and persistently develop and evolve exact action plans over time. It's important to develop a long-term plan for creating and sustaining an innovative culture. It helps to conduct ongoing learning events and to develop new resources and strategies as needed. Basically, this entails an ongoing process that ensures progress toward goals, modifications as needed, continuous improvement, the development of new learning tools as needed, and continual alignment and realignment with business objectives. From the beginning, institute a continuous process of planning, implementing, checking, refining, and acting upon needed improvements to your innovation strategy.

Don't expect to alter your organization's innovation capabilities overnight. But also don't get started down the road to innovation if you're not serious. Commitment to innovation means investing time, talent, money, and energy. Commitment also requires being prepared to stumble and to get back up. You must be willing to accept some failures and setbacks along the way. Like so many things in life, you'll only get as much in return from an innovation strategy as you are willing to invest. You can read every diet book you can find, but you won't lose any weight if you're turning the pages with one hand and eating chocolate-chip cookies with the other. If your commitment and investment are superficial or half-hearted, the people you lead will know. Your reward will be increased cynicism and skepticism, which are tough hurdles to clear.

4. Define what you mean by innovation

Your definition and outline of innovation will be different from those of your competitors. That doesn't matter. What does matter is that everyone in your organization or on your team understands what you mean by innovation – in the context of your business. It is not enough to simply write "innovation" in mission statements, corporate reports, or memos to managers and employees and expect them to know what to do next. All too often, that approach leaves everyone talking about innovation but responding with blank stares or vague approximations when asked what it means in terms of their daily performance.

You need to describe how innovation integrates into the fabric of your organization. You need to define innovation as it relates to your management structure, product or service development, process improvement, systems, customer service, and sales and marketing.

Creating and committing to a definition of innovation is the responsibility of leadership, but involving other people in that process can go a long way toward creating Linkage. However you approach this step, you must paint a vivid picture of what your organization will look and feel like when it is operating with an innovative culture. What mindsets must change? How will people think? What behaviors must change? What role will leaders play? What roles will your team play?

It is essential that you demonstrate visible and concrete support for what you want innovation to look like in day-to-day practice. That point is highlighted by a study of 350 executives from companies in fourteen industries done by Arthur D. Little Company. Six factors were cited as being most important to the successful implementation of any organizational change. The factors cited most often were:

- 95 percent – A clear vision of the proposed change
- 94 percent – Management support – through actions, not just words
- 90 percent – Measurable targets
- 83 percent – Doable targets
- 76 percent – The perception that the change will improve things
- 74 percent – Employee empowerment

People need to know, through words *and* actions, what you mean when you say, "We need to be more innovative." Acknowledge, recognize, and hold up examples of innovation success. And equally important, exemplify your tolerance for, and willingness to learn from, the nice-try innovation attempts that are not successful. People will be watching. What you do in the face of success and setbacks will say more about how you define innovation than any well-written decree.

5. Assess your innovation capabilities

Understanding your innovation capabilities is a useful way to focus your efforts and resources. Having made the commitment to becoming more innovative presents you with an immediate dilemma: you have limited resources. You simply can't do everything all at once. Where do you start? Which innovation efforts will generate the biggest return on your investment? What are the greatest obstacles and inhibitors to innovation and creativity that should be addressed first?

A measurement of your innovation capabilities allows you to pinpoint the specific and critical elements – the management systems, behaviors, work conditions, etc. – that discourage employees from achieving peak performance and make them unwilling or unable to take reasonable risks, generate ideas, and embrace change in ways that can augment the success of the company. With that information, you can zero in on the areas with the greatest potential for improving creativity and innovation.

Even if you believe you understand the organizational stimulants and barriers that are encouraging or inhibiting creativity and innovation, it is important to evaluate these elements objectively. The evaluation or assessment can be formal or informal. You can use outside resources or do the assessment internally. Getting an accurate assessment of the cultural elements, as well as of the individual styles and attributes that affect creativity and innovation, provides you with an innovation gap analysis showing where your organization is today, compared with the state of innovation you desire in the future. (A gap analysis is a process in which you list the present situation in one column, the desired situation in the other, and then focus on what lies between them – the gap – that currently prevents you and your team or organization from achieving the desired situation.)

Involving the people you lead in the process of discovering your innovation capabilities communicates your commitment to making innovation elemental – involving everyone, everywhere, every day. Respecting employees' concerns and ideas about what in the work environment fosters or inhibits creativity begins the process of getting them involved in the solution. It engenders buy-in and ownership.

Also, the outcomes of innovation capability assessments serve as a baseline against which your organization can measure results and target future specific strategies to enhance innovation. There is a widely accepted belief in business that what gets measured gets done. Measurement systems get attention, drive behavior, and lead to dramatic change.

Mike Simms, an executive with Wainwright Industries, used American Major League Baseball as an example of this phenomenon with an audience at a conference sponsored by the Association for Quality and Participation. In 1998, St. Louis Cardinals star Mark McGwire was chasing Roger Maris' thirty-seven-year-old single-season home run record, which many believed would never be topped.

"In St. Louis," he said, "hundreds of thousands of people who never cared about baseball tuned in to Mark McGwire because of the measures and the historical significance."

Keeping measures clear, significant, and team-oriented sharpens focus, Simms said, and has been instrumental in helping his Missouri-based metal stamping and machining company excel, including winning the Malcolm Baldrige National Quality Award from the US National Institute of Standards and Technology. "A team sandbagging the banks of a flooding river, for example, needs only two clear measures," Simms said, "the level of the water and the height of the wall."

Remember, this is a journey, not a destination. It's not a single initiative, a program of the month, or a quick fix. The value of auditing and measuring specific innovation goals is enhanced when repeated with groups of employees at designated intervals to measure progress toward creating an innovative culture. It's also important to acknowledge and appreciate the areas of your organization that are currently doing well in stimulating creativity and innovation. It is critical to build on that success. Setting out to become more innovative should not carry the message that everything being done today is wrong or not innovative.

6. Align structures and systems to support a culture of innovation

Culture is what people do when nobody is watching, which is why it can be such a challenging task to understand, define, communicate, and change it – and why so many people avoid dealing with it. However, ignoring it can sabotage everything else you do to foster innovation.

Many structures and systems shape an organization's culture. Its policies and procedures, management structures, and processes mold everything that happens in and around the organization. Therefore, becoming an innovative organization mandates a "systems-thinking" or holistic approach to the structuring of your organization and its systems. Every action and decision is connected.

We tend to understand this idea better as we begin to use more biological rather than mechanical metaphors to describe business. It helps to view companies as living organisms rather than machines with replaceable parts. The organization of the future will be a thinking and learning organization. In this paradigm, the organization will need, in the face of adversity or market change, to be able to think, adapt, respond, and remember – as an organizational whole – in order to anticipate and handle competitive threats.

As we said earlier, many experts in the human-resources field who focus on performance management have long argued that if you put good people into a bad system, the system will win almost every time. One classic dysfunctional behavior, for example, is for a management team to "talk" about innovation but to "walk" the status quo. Don't ask people to take risks in the name of needed change and then create systems that tell them any ideas they have must pass through a chain of command twelve layers thick, or that you "reward" failure with being fired.

Keep in mind that it is not just major policies and practices that can convey an innovation-deflating message. Little things can cause major problems. One client organization, a governmental-contract administration firm, asked us to help facilitate a merger of three divisions by creating a change- and innovation-friendly culture with a hundred of its middle-management team. In preparing for the project, we quickly learned from some in the target audience that there was considerable skepticism, even cynicism, about top management's intentions for this initiative.

The talk in announcing this project had been all about the top-leadership team wanting change, creativity, empowerment, and increased risk-taking in the ranks. The walk, however, had included recent changes in guidelines that had cut certain managers' acquisitions authority from $10,000 to $1,000. The new bureaucracy even prohibited the three merging divisions from planning their own company picnics, apparently out of concern they might not do things the same way. Mixed messages such as these usually end up with messy results.

Another key to building and maintaining cultural and management systems that support innovation is to understand that they grow out of a sense of individual and organizational purpose. Purpose acts as the bond that keeps individuals and organizations working together; the stronger the purpose, the more cohesive the effort. Purpose provides guidance for day-to-day decision making because you can anchor yourself by regularly asking, "Does this particular action support our purpose?"

Knowledge workers need meaningful work. Innovative organizations need meaningful work. If your view of the purpose of your organization is limited to what you make or the services you provide, you face a major obstacle in becoming more innovative and therefore more successful. Why are you in business?

Why is your organization managed the way it is? Why do you do the work you do?

Jim Collins is co-author of the book *Built to Last*, which chronicles the history and inner workings of some of the most successful and most enduring companies in the United States. His research, he says, shows a correlation between purpose, longevity, and prosperity.

"Concentrating on products or services is a trap," he told *Inc.* magazine. "It's not that what a company makes is irrelevant; only that we'll see more companies finding their identity in terms of their core purpose.... It's more important than ever to define yourself in terms of what you stand for rather than what you make, because what you make is going to become outmoded faster than it has at any time in the past. [So,] you hang on to the idea of who you are as a company, and you focus not on what you do but what you could do."

Collins used Motorola and Zenith as examples. In the 1950s, they were competitors making television sets. Zenith, he said, saw its purpose as making TVs. Motorola saw its purpose as finding ways to apply technology for the benefit of society. Zenith, once a household name, has almost disappeared from memory. Motorola has had its ups and downs but has been one of the world's most successful companies.

If you take this kind of a broad systems-thinking perspective to leading innovation, you will be forced to look beyond individual mistakes, personalities, and events to understand what *underlies* problems. Instead of providing a simple way to affix blame, the systems approach guides you to look for ways to fix the underlying structures that foster undesirable individual action and to create the conditions that encourage certain kinds of behavior and performance. Systems thinkers grasp a profound insight: systems shape behavior. Put good people into a bad system and the system wins, but put good people into a good system and everybody wins.

It makes no sense to push innovation as a corporate priority but then fail to ruthlessly evaluate every structure and system for its alignment with your strategy for fostering innovation.

7. Maintain and reinforce the innovation momentum

It's vital to continually evaluate what's working and what's not when it comes to efforts to foster innovation. Training needs will change. The effectiveness of rewards and incentives will change. Your definition of innovation will likely evolve. But you will know you are on the right path when the predominant philosophy is, "If something's broke, fix it; if something isn't broke, fix it." You'll know the organization is evolving into being perpetually innovative when you understand that what's working today won't be working tomorrow in a radically changing marketplace.

The competitive advantage of having an entire organization operate based on innovation-driven goals is significant. To reach these goals, you must nurture a mindset and workplace in which people feel safe and valued. You must create an environment that demands commitment, not compliance. Then it is up to each individual to take personal responsibility for, and reap the benefits of, contributing within that culture.

The S.E.L.V.E.S. Thinking Model

Use our S.E.L.V.E.S. Thinking Model for innovation and problem solving, but also for discussing strategy, dealing with conflict, etc. S.E.L.V.E.S stands for Statement, Emotion, Logic, Vision, Exploration, and Solutions. Using this model will help you organize your thoughts, guide discussions, uncover problems, widen thinking, and expedite decision making.

When using S.E.L.V.E.S., it is important to have your group agree to work on a single step at a time, discussing a given question from the same perspective. That is, when you are dealing with the Logic of a situation, don't allow your group's discussion to lapse into an Emotional debate. If you have already adequately discussed the feelings people have about the situation, remind them you have agreed to move on to exploring the facts. Or, if the feelings are still strong, agree that you will come back to them after you have dealt with the Logic phase.

The six steps don't have to be used in sequence. In fact, it can be very effective to revisit steps regularly. For example, you may carefully consider the Emotion and Logic of your Situation but need to revisit these elements as you Explore and decide upon Solutions. S.E.L.V.E.S. is especially effective for organizing an agenda for a meeting or a timeline for a project.

Statement

This step gets everyone on the same page in understanding the challenge or opportunity and assures you are working on the right problem. Search out the underlying circumstances and elements you must deal with that accurately define the problem or explain the parameters of the decision you must make. Ask:

• What is the situation? • What will be the challenges? • Where are the pains? • Are there opportunities? What are they? Where? • Who is involved? Why? • What are our strengths? Weaknesses? • What are the threats inherent in the situation?

Emotion

Because emotions can sometimes overrule logic, it's important to address emotion early in the process. It's essential to uncover both the positive and negative emotions about how people feel – or might feel – about the problem or situation. Ask:

• What are the emotions that will help or hinder the process of finding a solution? • Why is solving the problem important? • What are the positive aspects of addressing this situation? • What if we don't do anything at all? • Will solving the problem be good news? • How will people react during the problem-solving process? • How will they feel or react once the problem is solved? • What if it doesn't work? • Why wouldn't it work?

Logic

It's important that everyone recognize the objective, factual aspects of your discussion. Ensure there is ample opportunity to expose differing interpretations of the facts, consider the strengths or weaknesses of your data, and so forth. Ask:

• What are the facts and figures of the situation? • Where is the data incomplete, open to interpretation, or reliable? • What's unquestionably true? • What does your data tell you? • What does research by others say? • When you look at the situation from an objective point of view, what do you see? • What's real? What proof do you have? • What are the market numbers? • What facts do you know about the competition, the context, or external factors relative to the challenge?

Vision

Vision is an expression of what the problem will look like once it's solved. It is a clear picture of the endpoint you are shooting for when the problem is resolved. Don't confuse it with your organization's grand vision or mission. Ask:

• Once we solve this problem, what will things look like? • Can we measure the success of the solution? How? • Who would be doing what? • What would be done differently? • What new technologies would be used? • What would customers be doing or saying?

Exploration

Exploration is the point when you begin to deliberately think about and collect possible solutions to a problem. Exploration involves doing research, experimenting, brainstorming, and collaborating with others who may have ideas to contribute and/or have a stake in resolving the problem. Ask:

• Have you asked and answered the question "why?" enough times to describe the underlying cause or causes of the problem? • Do we need to refine our problem statement? • Do we understand all the root causes? • Who has information, influence, or position to contribute to the various possible solutions? • Who needs to know about the various possible solutions?

Solutions

In this action step, your team weighs all the possible solutions identified in the Exploration stage. Repeat whatever S.E.L.V.E.S. steps are needed, and decide upon the best alternatives. Ask:

• What is going to be done? • Who is going to do it? • What are the timeframes, resources, planning issues, communications issues, logistics, people power, and finances involved?

As a leader you are already accustomed, no doubt, to taking large challenges and breaking them into actionable "pieces." When you are committed to creating a culture of innovation, your ability to do so will be invaluable. So will a dose of patience, humor, flexibility and empathy as you lead this effort. It surely won't come overnight, but with dedication you will see results.

Chapter 13

Decision-Making and Prioritization Tools

The whole problem with the world is that fools and fanatics are always so certain of themselves, and the wiser people so full of doubt.

—Bertrand Russell

Brainstorming and idea generation can be seductive. It's fun. It's high energy. It's gratifying to test your creativity and to see a long list of the results. But some of the hardest work of leading innovation happens when you have to sort through your ideas, decide upon the best alternatives, build consensus, and then put your ideas into action.

Much of what we have shared with you so far about LOOP Leadership has been designed to help you expand your thinking. We've challenged you to look at your problems and opportunities differently, and we've encouraged you to pour more creative energy into the hunt for good ideas. You are now at the point in the "ideation process," however, where you must begin narrowing your options. The tools and ideas in this chapter will help you do just that by showing you some effective ways to manage multitudes of ideas, zero in on best alternatives, and champion ideas into action.

A word of caution: When you turn the corner from the divergent phase of ideation, which encourages free association, suspension of judgment, and anything-goes-thinking, groups often hit what Sam Kaner calls "the groan zone" in his book, *Facilitator's Guide to Participatory Decision-Making*.

You know the place. People become irritated and impatient with each other. Discussions can get polarized. Conversations go in circles. Frustration builds until somebody with a persuasive and powerful personality wins out, or the group tires and gives up, resulting in a defeatist, let's-just-decide-something-and-move-on attitude.

Five guidelines for turning ideas into action

Our goal is to get you through the groan zone and into the next steps of productive and creative problem solving. As you work with the specific tools we describe in this chapter, keep these five guidelines and reminders in mind. They will help you build better consensus and avoid breakdowns in collaboration during the ideation process phases of the convergence, idea selection, and implementation.

Guideline #1: define specific solution criteria first

This may be the most important and most frequently overlooked step in effective evaluation and prioritization of ideas. You must be able to answer the question, "How will we know if an idea is good?" Based on what criteria will you

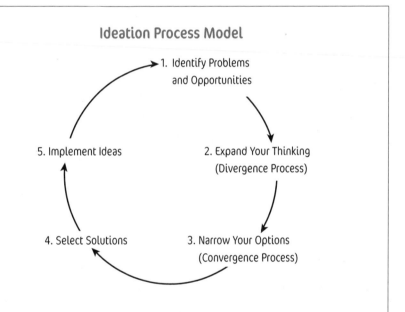

Ideation Process Model

1. Identify Problems and Opportunities

2. Expand Your Thinking (Divergence Process)

3. Narrow Your Options (Convergence Process)

4. Select Solutions

5. Implement Ideas

The ideation process begins with identifying the problem or opportunity you must address (step 1). From there, you need to expand your thinking, fanning out creatively to generate as many ideas as possible without evaluating or assessing their viability (step 2). The work gets a little tougher when you must converge your thought process and begin to narrow your options (step 3), choose which ideas to implement (step 4), and then do the actual work to put those ideas into action (step 5, which naturally will branch into lots of other steps).

judge one idea against another? In brainstorming, you deliberately suspend judgment. But during the prioritization and decision phases of ideation you must make judgments, and you can't do that without clearly delineated criteria. Is cost a criterion? Ease of use? Quality? Availability? Time to market?

Most likely you will gauge with multiple sets of criteria, but not all of the factors will carry the same weight in your decision making. Some criteria will be more important than others. You can determine criteria on your own, or you can make that part of the discussion and teamwork. In either case, the criteria must be based on a deep understanding of the desired end state to which the solution is to be applied, whether it's customer needs, market potential, performance requirements, financial targets, or something else.

Guideline #2: the process isn't linear

Going from problems to solutions is an iterative process. At any point in the process new insights and information may dictate the need to circle back to an earlier step. It's common for a group to be engaged in convergent thinking and homing in on a potential solution when they realize the original problem or opportunity needs to be redefined. Or occasionally a blinding flash of the obvious allows the group to skip several steps. Those are rare but beautiful moments. Keep an open mind throughout the entire ideation process and continue to practice the mindsets discussed earlier in chapter 11.

Guideline #3: separate the idea from its "author"

This is a challenging but extremely fruitful facilitation technique. The goal is to avoid applying positive and negative "spins" or evaluations on ideas based on who offers them. You'll see lots of sources of spin. Does a newcomer's or consultant's idea have more or less appeal than the idea of a loyal, long-term employee in your organization? Does hierarchy, office address or location, or age play a role? Separating the idea from the author accomplishes several important things when helping a group prioritize and evaluate ideas. It reduces the tendency to make assumptions and inferences about what others' agendas might be, and it keeps people focused on the merit of an idea relative to the problem or opportunity. This guideline also fosters greater participation of everyone involved and helps create an environment in which difficult issues and different perspectives can be raised. Listening to each other's ideas – without the drawbacks of perceived personal or political intentions or other baggage – promotes mutual understanding of, and shared responsibility for, finding the best solutions.

Guideline #4: the number one (and number two) cause of problems – solutions

Today's solutions are ultimately tomorrow's problems. This is the natural cycle of problem solving, and it is why we represent our Ideation Process Model as a circle. Living by this philosophy drives continuous improvement. With this mindset, people are less frustrated when "problems" arise. It helps them stay more focused on the opportunities for improvement that are inherent in the natural cycle of change. Solutions are not the end of the road. They are the beginning of a new cycle.

Another problem with solutions is that if you and your team move too *fast* to them, without taking time to really make sure you've identified or scoped the problems fully, your solutions may be partial and therefore even more short lived – and thus require revisiting even sooner. For you as a leader, it's a delicate task to promote the creative search for solutions but to insist that everyone agrees on what you're solving, before opening the floodgates!

Guideline #5: think ahead about possible derailment

When a group is settling on an idea or action plan, it is useful – but sometimes painful – to ask, "What could get in the way of our implementing this idea or action?" The answer may help the group begin to formulate the key issues or potential obstacles that must be thought through in order to get wider buy-in to move the idea forward. This question can also uncover a key issue or root cause that has not yet been brought up – requiring redefining the problem or opportunity. This can be frustrating and tiresome, but it is better to learn about problems earlier than later.

Prioritizing and evaluating ideas

One of the first steps in sorting through lots of ideas is to categorize or reduce the volume to a manageable level. The following two processes will help in organizing your group's ideas.

1. Affinity Grouping Tool

Affinity Grouping is a simple but effective process that allows small teams to sort and organize ideas, information, or data based on the relationships among the items – their affinity for one another. This process will help your team make sense of complex and unwieldy issues by emphasizing connections between issues or ideas that they might not otherwise see. Affinity Grouping is a natural way to foster emergent thinking, promote consensus building, and generate more creative solutions. The process is both creative and rational. Affinity Groupings are most useful when:

- The problem or opportunity is difficult to understand.
- The problem or opportunity is uncertain, disorganized, or overwhelming.
- A brainstorming session has created a large volume of ideas.
- The situation requires the involvement and support of the group.

Steps in Creating an Affinity Grouping:
1. Write each idea on a separate index card or Post-it Note.
2. Post the ideas where everyone can view and work with them. You can post them all at once and then begin the process of creating affinity groups, or you can ask people to place ideas or issues one at a time and, in turn, to create the groupings. (This process works best in groups of six to eight people. If your group is larger, form subgroups to work with subsets of ideas and issues first.)

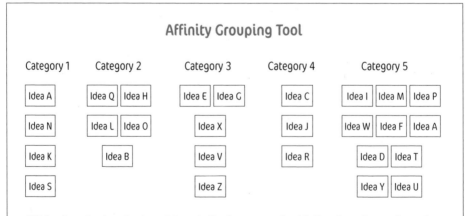

Affinity Grouping Tool

Category 1	Category 2	Category 3	Category 4	Category 5
Idea A	Idea Q / Idea H	Idea E / Idea G	Idea C	Idea I / Idea M / Idea P
Idea N	Idea L / Idea O	Idea X	Idea J	Idea W / Idea F / Idea A
Idea K	Idea B	Idea V	Idea R	Idea D / Idea T
Idea S		Idea Z		Idea Y / Idea U

Affinity Grouping is a simple, quick, and effective process for thinking through complex and unwieldy issues. The basic challenge is to recognize the interconnections between issues or ideas, organize them visually so they can be compared, and then identify the underlying themes.

3. Ask the group members to use their intuition as well as their rational and logical thinking to rearrange the notes into groupings of similar ideas and issues. Ask people to work silently in the beginning to prevent "group think" from overriding potentially unusual or interesting affinities. It's okay if the notes for certain ideas and issues are moved between groupings during this process. If you notice an idea being moved repeatedly, duplicate it and place it in more than one group. If a particular idea or issue becomes contentious, set it aside to deal with it later during open discussion.

4. After all ideas and issues are clustered, discuss the groupings, clarify questions, and redistribute any ideas and issues as needed. Now develop headers or categories that most accurately reflect the theme of each grouping. It is usually during this step of Affinity Grouping that you gain the greatest benefits of the technique. It is also the point where your facilitation skills will be most tested. The dialogue about how and why issues and ideas should be organized a certain way is what leads to breakthroughs. Dialogue promotes shared understanding and unique combinations, so let it flow as long as it's productive. Generally, it is useful to limit the total number of categories to five or ten.

2. Multi-Voting Tool

Multi-voting (or dot voting) is a technique for quickly narrowing a wide array of potential or competing ideas. Each person gets to cast several votes to help select among many ideas or issues. It is most effective when combined with follow-up discussions about the reasons and motivations for people's choices.

Steps in Multi-Voting:
1. **Define and clarify ideas:** Clarify and agree on important terms. List them on flip charts or other similar media. Eliminate redundancies in your list, but do not allow critical discussion or debate of the ideas at this point. Describe each idea in enough detail that participants can make informed selections.
2. **Decide on your appropriate number of "top" ideas:** Decide on the number of ideas you would like to end up with for further discussion and development. Depending upon time available and size of the group, the best range is often three to five ideas. More than ten defeats the purpose of the method.

Multi-Voting Tool

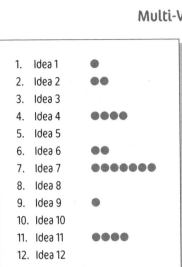

The group selects ideas four, seven, and eleven for further discussion and exploration.

Although you'll seldom want to base a business decision solely on a vote, this is largely a democratic process that allows all stakeholders to have an equal voice in determining the comparative value of competing ideas and issues. This process is most effective when you allow time to discuss the reasoning behind the votes.

3. **Voting:** Count the total number of ideas. If there are fewer than twenty, give each person the right to cast three to seven votes. If you have twenty or more ideas, give each person a number of votes equal to approximately one-third of the total number of ideas. Going beyond twenty votes becomes unmanageable. You can vote by show of hands, or by having people put check marks, initials (if anonymity isn't important) or sticky paper dots beside the items they vote for. Have everyone vote. Each person can vote only once for any single idea. Eliminate the bottom one-third of the ideas – those receiving the least number of votes. Repeat the process until you narrow the list to your desired number of ideas. Discuss the ideas between rounds for clarity purposes, if necessary, but resist critical discussion about specific ideas until you narrow the list to your desired number of ideas.

4. **Options:** If you start with fewer ideas than the number of people voting, you can quickly reduce the list by giving each person the same number of votes as the number of desired "top choices." For example, if you want the group to arrive at a list of their top seven ideas, give each person seven votes. If the top seven choices are not obvious after the first round of votes, repeat a round of voting with only those items that received a "tie vote" on the previous round. Another option is to use different colored dots to represent a hi-

erarchy of choice. For example, red for top choices and blue for all other votes. We have used different colored dots to represent different functions, customers, or market segments in order to determine whether there is any bias depending upon perspective. Finally, contrary to the method above, you can use "intensity" voting. Allow people to give an idea more than one or all of their votes. This usually results in creating shorter lists of top choices more quickly, but a possible drawback is the voting can be skewed by extreme points of view.

Deciding on ideas

Deciding on the best ideas requires a clear understanding and consensus on solution criteria. Once you have decided how you will judge the merits of an idea, you can begin the dialogue about which ideas have the best potential for success. For the most part, your evaluation of an idea will center on objective and quantifiable measures. But don't prematurely dismiss ideas that feel right even though they don't initially match your criteria. With a little work and data collection, these ideas might be worth saving. Here are five techniques that really pay off.

1. Simple Paired Comparison Tool

Simple paired comparison is a method of prioritizing a list of ideas, decision criteria, attributes, etc. by comparing items on a one-to-one basis. The advantage of this process is that it allows you to analyze a number of items two at a time, which is easier than comparing many items at once. Simple paired comparison works well when comparing a relatively small number of items, but becomes more cumbersome with longer lists.

Steps for Simple Paired Comparison:
1. List all of the items to be compared. If the ideas are lengthy, assign a letter or keyword to each idea.
2. Make sure everyone knows what criteria define a "good" idea. In our example, "tastiness" is the criterion. Consider how the results might differ if the criterion were "nutritional value" or "portability."
3. Create a grid with each idea or item as both a column and row header.
4. Block out the squares that represent items being compared against themselves or that repeat pairings.

Simple Paired Comparison Tool

	Apple	Banana	Carrot	Donut	Cookie	Yogurt	Orange	Chips	Score
Apple		Apple	Apple	Donut	Cookie	Apple	Orange	Apple	4
Banana			Banana	Donut	Cookie	Yogurt	Orange	Chips	1
Carrot				Donut	Cookie	Yogurt	Orange	Carrot	1
Donut					Cookie	Yogurt	Donut	Donut	5
Cookie						Cookie	Cookie	Cookie	7
Yogurt							Yogurt	Yogurt	5
Orange								Orange	4
Chips									1

In this example of a simple paired comparison, all eight items are compared against each other with the criterion of *tastiness*, using the snack listings in the left column and top row of the grid to organize the voting. The winner in each comparison is recorded in the inner columns and rows, and then tallied in the far right column. Cookie is the clear overall winner, chosen as more tasty than each of the other seven snacks on the list.

5. Start with the first row. Compare that item against each item listed in the columns – one at a time – selecting which item or idea is "better," according to your agreed-upon criteria. Put that item (or letter) in the corresponding box in the grid. Continue until you compare each item against all the others.

6. Add up how many times each idea was selected when compared to the other ideas and record the total next to the idea under the score column. The item appearing most frequently is the top choice. The second highest score is the second best idea, etc.

2. Weighted Paired Comparison Tool

Weighted paired comparison is very similar to simple paired comparison, but incorporates an element of importance or weight when comparing one idea against another. This can be particularly beneficial when the ideas or items are more subjective.

Steps for Weighted Paired Comparison:

1. Set up your list, criteria, and grid as described in simple paired comparison.

Weighted Paired Comparison Tool

	Cost	Mileage	Style	Comfort	Resale	Maintenance	Cargo Capacity	Score
Cost		Mileage 2	Cost 2	Cost 1	Resale 1	Maintenance 3	Cost 2	5
Mileage			Mileage 3	Mileage 2	Mileage 2	Mileage 1	Mileage 3	13
Style				Comfort 2	Resale 2	Maintenance 3	Cargo 2	0
Comfort					Resale 1	Maintenance 2	Cargo 1	2
Resale						Maintenance 1	Resale 2	4
Maintenance							Main. 3	12
Cargo Cap.								3

Importance Factor: Low = 1 Medium = 2 High = 3

Weighted paired comparison, like the simple paired comparison, is a process for comparing multiple items against each other one pair at a time. In this case, the grid is used to help make a decision about buying a car based on seven valuable features. The difference in the two tools is the addition of the 1 to 3 importance factor in the weighted comparison. In this example, "mileage" and "maintenance" with scores of 13 and 12 are the winners in these comparisons.

2. Compare items against each other. Select which item is better according to your agreed-upon criteria *and* assign an importance factor to the *difference* in merit between the two:

- 1 = not much difference in merit
- 2 = some difference in merit
- 3 = very different merit

For example, if you select item A over item B and you believe the difference in the merit of the ideas is only minimal, write A-1 in the corresponding box in the grid. If A is much better than B, record the score as A-3.

1. Repeat the one-to-one comparison with all the items on the list, recording weighted scores for each winner.
2. Add up the total score for each idea and record it next to the idea in the score column.

3. Screening Tool

A screening grid is a useful way to perform a preliminary assessment of a list of ideas against two predetermined decision criteria. This technique is best with a list of up to twenty ideas, unless you can complete the process in multiple sessions.

Steps for Creating a Screening Grid:

1. Ask the group to decide on the two most important and relevant decision criteria. Each criterion may be a single measure or a set of measures, grouped together or summarized in a meaningful phrase.
2. Arrange the criteria along a two-axis grid, and use a scale with rankings of

Screening Tool

		Low	Medium	High
Value	High	Idea 1	Idea 6	Idea 12 Idea 8
	Medium	Idea 11	Idea 2	Idea 7
	Low	Idea 4 Idea 10	Idea 3 Idea 9	Idea 5
		Low	Medium	High

Cost

Use a screening grid to compare ideas against two important criteria. In this example, twelve ideas are evaluated based on cost and value. Idea 1, which has a high value and a low cost, is probably the best idea of the twelve. Idea 5, with a high cost and a low value, is probably the worst of the ideas.

high, medium, and low for each criterion to create a three-by-three grid.

3. Assess each idea subjectively on how well it meets each of the two criteria. Write each idea in one of the nine boxes of the grid, according to its ranking.

4. Ideas that score highest in criteria are the top choices.

4. Effort-Impact Tool

The effort-impact grid is a simple but useful tool to evaluate ideas quickly and efficiently. You can rate the effort and impact on a high versus low scale, creating a two-by-two grid, or on a high, medium, low scale, creating a three-by-three grid. Discuss and place each idea into one of the boxes of the grid based on your evaluation of the potential impact of the idea and what effort or resources would be required to implement the idea.

*   *Low Effort/High Impact Ideas:* These ideas are cheap and easy to implement and produce significant improvement or benefits. Obviously, these are the ideas you want to implement immediately.
*   *High Effort/High Impact Ideas:* These ideas are difficult or expensive to implement but produce significant improvement or benefits. They will require additional planning and marshalling of resources. Further refinement of these ideas is necessary until you can get the return on investment high enough for them to become a priority. These ideas need persistent revisiting.

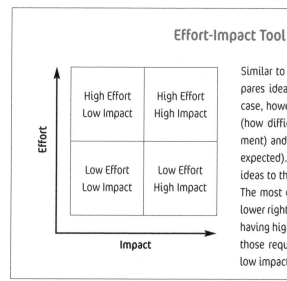

Effort-Impact Tool

High Effort Low Impact	High Effort High Impact
Low Effort Low Impact	Low Effort High Impact

Effort (vertical axis) — Impact (horizontal axis)

Similar to a screening grid, this tool compares ideas based on two criteria. In this case, however, the criteria are fixed: effort (how difficult will this idea be to implement) and impact (what payoff should be expected). Use adhesive notes to assign ideas to the appropriate spots on the grid. The most desirable ideas are those in the lower right – those requiring low effort and having high impact. The least desirable are those requiring high effort but promising low impact.

- *Low Effort/Low Impact Ideas:* These ideas are cheap or easy to implement, but produce minimal improvement or benefits. You may or may not want to implement them – just because an idea is cheap or easy doesn't mean it's smart to execute it. Find ways to improve the impact with minimal or no increase in resource allotment.

- *High Effort/Low Impact Ideas:* These ideas are difficult or expensive to implement and produce minimal improvement or benefits. Clearly, these ideas are *not* ones you want to implement. But as we have emphasized before, play with these ideas and build on them in ways that can result in reducing the resources required, increasing the return, or transforming them into something useful yet totally unexpected. Some leaders keep a file of these to review periodically, in case changed conditions alter their ranking dramatically.

5. Risk Analysis Tool

Innovation by its very nature involves risk. Some of the uncertainty and unknowns can be resolved early in the ideation process. Other ambiguities will remain throughout the process. And often, before an idea can get serious consideration, the risks must be explored. Rather than just crossing your fingers and hoping that everything will work out somehow, it makes sense to analyze and reduce the risks as early as possible. In our work with clients, we often analyze risk on two levels: the *probability of occurrence,* or the likelihood an event might happen, and the *severity of impact,* or how bad it would be if the event were to happen. You can use this simple method to assess and prioritize risks on these continuums.

Steps in Risk Analysis:

1. Make a list of all the uncertainties, things that could go wrong, or other problematic issues that could affect the idea and its success.

2. For each issue, rate the probability of occurrence and severity of impact as high, medium, or low.

3. Give a score of five to any issue that is high probability or high severity. Give a three to issues that are medium probability or severity. Score a one for those with low probability and severity. Derive the risk score by multiplying *severity times probability*, which will produce a number between one and twenty-five.

Risk Analysis Tool

	1	3	5
5	Medium (5)	High (15)	High (25)
3	Low (3)	Medium (9)	High (15)
1	Low (1)	Low (3)	Medium (5)

Severity (vertical axis)

Probability (horizontal axis): 1, 3, 5

Risk analysis is useful for thinking ahead about what might go wrong in implementing new ideas and the potential negative outcomes that could result from those problems. In this example, risks you believe would have a very severe impact and that are highly probable earn scores of 25 and fall into the upper right corner of this grid. Risks you believe would have a low impact and that are improbable earn scores of 1 and fall into the lower left corner of this grid.

4. Categorize each issue according to its overall risk. High risk items are those with scores fifteen or twenty-five. Medium risk items are those with scores of five or nine. And low risk items are those with scores of one or three. Creating a two-axis grid with three squares along each axis is a useful way to be able to visualize how the risks compare.
5. Discuss what can be done to reduce risk in the high-risk issues that may arise in the future.

Championing and selling ideas

Few things are more counterproductive to innovation than shooting someone's idea out of the sky. It's disheartening and frustrating to have ideas met with apathy, resistance, or outright rejection. It kills excitement and passion, both critical ingredients for creativity.

Ideas, even good ideas, need champions to thrive. And one of the important things you need to remember about being a champion of ideas is that new ideas, by definition, are unsettling. New ideas require change. They challenge the status quo.

Implementing new ideas entails embracing risk and the potential for failure, and it also means contending with one of the most powerful forces in organizations: inertia. New ideas demand action and resources (time, money, personnel) and that usually means a reshuffling of priorities. All of this will probably trigger resistance, fear, and skepticism. Understanding and anticipating these organizational and human realities can strengthen your resolve when floating and supporting ideas even in the roughest waters.

Your job, as a champion of ideas, is to tilt the playing field in favor of fresh thinking. To successfully implement new initiatives, you must elevate the importance and urgency of what is being proposed in relation to all of the other important and urgent things that key people must deal with. That's not an easy task, especially when the benefits may be long-term or appear intangible.

Here are some guidelines for building commitment and support for ideas:

- **Prevent resistance and objections:** Think in terms of preventing objections rather than overcoming them. Look at ideas from the perspective of others to reduce the chances of them saying, "No." Once people make it known that they reject an idea, it is much harder for them to reverse their positions later and still save face. They will require a great deal more persuasion down the road if they have previously rejected an idea.

- **Involve key stakeholders early:** Get preliminary input and advice in the early stages of idea development. It is better to involve key stakeholders as an idea is being developed than to present a fully developed idea without understanding their perspectives. It is best to have done your due diligence with each stakeholder separately before presenting to them as a group. Develop an understanding and relationship with each stakeholder as it relates to an idea. This can be more challenging than it sounds. In the early stages of advocating a new idea, you may not relish the task of eliciting opposition in order to deal successfully with it. But it's well worth doing.

- **Seek to understand:** Spend less time convincing and telling others about an idea – especially key stakeholders – and more time getting advice and input. Any successful salesperson will tell you that selling requires asking good questions and listening more than talking. Your questions should help *you* better understand the big picture from the perspective of others and the implications of the idea relative to their priorities, challenges, and objectives. Their answers will help *them* create a case for acting on the idea. People are hesitant to dispute their own data. Learn and understand stakeholder needs, and then communicate the benefits of new ideas in terms of these needs. This is not about manipulation, but true understanding and empathy. What are the benefits to your customers, the business, your organization, and key stakeholders? How should they affect your thinking?

- **Share the ownership:** It is far more important to get a good idea implemented than it is to keep track of who should get credit. By the time a good idea is fully developed and implemented, it should be nearly impossible to determine any single owner of the idea. Done right, your idea should have as many fingerprints on it as you can get. This does more than just show your altruistic tendencies. When you enlist many co-owners in the development of your idea you simultaneously build a band of advocates, a small sales force that is passionately committed to seeing the idea implemented. It is far more effective to have many champions of an idea than to go it alone.

- **Be authentic.** People can tell whether you have the best interest of the business at heart or you are on a self-serving drive to have a pet project advanced. Take the time to understand an idea in the context of the overall objectives and priorities of the larger organization. What may seem like a great idea from your vantage point could be trivial, or even a possible disaster, when viewed from a broader organizational perspective. Be willing to modify and even subjugate your interests if necessary for the greater good of the overall business. As people come to understand that you think like this, they will be much more willing to follow your lead when you advance ideas that you strongly believe are in the best interest of your organization.

Committing to action

All the planning in the world is useless without action, and action doesn't usually happen without commitment. As you know, commitment is not something you can mandate; you've got to earn it. Using LOOP Leadership will get you earnest support. Commitment to action, if you have involved people effectively along the way, is a natural extension of the Plans phase. But check on people's commitment regularly during this phase by asking them explicitly what they will do to drive ideas forward, and by when. Then follow up: check back and hold people accountable for delivering on their commitments.

After a brainstorming and planning session, we often ask people to write "Dear Boss" letters to whomever they report to. We ask them to describe the specific actions they plan to take within a specific timeframe and the payoffs they expect. We work with their leaders to follow up with them regularly to see what support they need, what progress is being made, and what else can be done to help meet these goals.

Your own commitment must match, if not exceed, what you hope to get from the people you lead. If you pair your commitment with your team's, you have a far greater chance of getting where you want to go and everyone coming out a winner.

Chapter 14

Destination Innovation?

A journey of a thousand miles begins with a single step.

—Chinese Proverb

Leading innovation is a tough task. Perhaps the most difficult bit of reality to contend with is that, once you get "there," you're not really "there" at all.

The quest for innovation is never-ending. For every one thing you do right in creating a workplace where people can excel so your organization can thrive, two things will surely change about your market, industry, customers, technology, finances, regulatory requirements, and people.

So why is leading innovation so tough? Why does the idea of innovation create so much fear?

- There's no simple formula or cookbook for innovation.
- Innovation requires acceptance of failure. That's not an easy sell, but an organization not failing is not innovating.
- Innovation requires a long-term perspective. An obsession with quarterly returns won't open the way to innovative new ideas, markets, strategies products, or services.
- Innovation can't merely be assigned. As a leader, you must demonstrate – through clear actions – your personal commitment to creativity and change.
- Innovation is a concept that is easy to love in theory, but when faced in reality, it requires courage to put in practice.
- There are risks and costs, but no guarantees.

The greatest risk in leading innovation, however, is to stand still and not innovate. Chances are, your biggest competitor in five years – no matter what industry you're in or what job you do – will probably be someone not even in your business today.

The greatest risk you may face as a leader personally, or as an organization, is putting too much of your energy into holding on to what you have or doing what you have always done – only faster.

The research Clayton Christensen did for his book, *The Innovator's Dilemma*, showed this kind of "good management" was the most powerful reason leading firms failed to stay atop their industries. Leading firms lost their front-runner positions because they riveted their attention on responding to existing customer needs and demands, Christensen says, instead of also paying attention to ideas and systems he labeled as "disruptive technologies." They were content to tweak their current success.

One of the great challenges of modern society is to learn to let go of what we already know and what we already have in order to get where we've never been and to achieve what has never been done.

The payoffs of creating an innovative workforce

Why is leading innovation so rewarding? What happens when you do let go of the status quo? What do you get when you commit to unraveling the rocket science of leadership by getting the people you lead eagerly engaged in pouring all their talent and creativity into their work? You get a team willing to do some unusual things. They will:

Go for broke

Competition moves too fast to be timid or cautious. Hustle – anticipation, speed, mobility, nimbleness – needs to become the hallmark of people's normal, everyday operating style. Abraham Lincoln once said, "Things may come to those who wait, but only the things left by those who hustle."

Create destruction

Pablo Picasso explained this seeming oxymoron when he said, "To create, you must first destroy." It's essential to mess with success. If it isn't broke . . . break it. Nothing lasts forever. Instead of idly standing by while obsolescence sets in, you want people to take the initiative to break old habits, break with tradition, and break the mold.

Leap before looking

In a world in which time is measured in nanoseconds, indecision is fatal more often than mistakes. Playing it safe is dangerous. Windows of opportunity open and shut quickly. Intuition is a key decision-making skill because of the role it can play in knowing when to analyze and when to act. Helen Keller put it this way, "Security is mostly a superstition. Avoiding danger is no safer in the long run than outright exposure. Life is either a daring adventure or nothing."

Fire themselves

With the demise of the traditional lifetime employment contract – "Do a good job and you're entitled to a job for life" – it's a fundamental mistake for people to think of themselves as working for someone else. You want an environment in which people "mentally" fire themselves and think more independently, assuming personal responsibility for their actions, the value they add, and their career and skill development. They work for the customer, not the company. The winning attitude is "I'm on the verge of being fired every day. If I'm not, I'm not doing my job. If I cease to push the envelope, I've failed."

Disturb the peace

The status quo won't create growth. You have to question everything, especially the how-we've-always-done-things-in-the-past practices. Most of us spend a lifetime conforming and trying to fit in. But predictable, conventional, and controlled workplaces and work routines are woefully inadequate for accommodating the freshness, originality, vitality, and passion needed to remain on top tomorrow. Robert Frost once said in an interview, "Thinking isn't agreeing or disagreeing. That's voting."

Learn like crazy

Just as an organization's willingness to accept the status quo is an obstacle to growth, an individual's acceptance of the status quo in personal development is a path to career obsolescence. Lifelong learning is required, not optional, for personal success. It is critical to help people make a habit of learning, unlearning, and relearning. And part of learning is the ability to cherish the learning inherent in failures. Thomas J. Barlow put it this way, "Even in the space age, the most important space is between the ears."

Lighten up

Laughter is a great resource. Not only does it help in relaxing and tapping creativity, it inspires reflection on personal passions and purpose, which influences performance. Lose the mentality that having fun and working hard are mutually exclusive events. Clarence Darrow said, "If you lose the power to laugh, you lose the power to think."

Final hopes and recommendations

At the outset of *Leading Innovation*, we said we had three hopes for what we would share on these pages:

1. To raise your awareness about what it takes to create and foster an environment of innovation.
2. To stimulate your thinking about the innovations and changes you can make in your leadership style.
3. To provide a framework, models, tools, stories, resources, insights, and inspiration you can use to create your own unique action plans for leading innovation and creating a workplace where people can excel so your organization can thrive.

We warned you we weren't promising any simple answers. No silver bullets. No formulas. No prescriptions. No step-by-step instructions. No scripts.

We've worked hard to organize our thinking in a way we believe is most useful for you. You now have enough to begin implementing LOOP Leadership. But this is when your hard work truly begins. Your leadership situation is unique, and so must be your application of these ideas and principles. The good news, which we've been emphasizing since page one, is that you are not alone. Our message, in its most elemental form is this: *Get people involved.* All of our experience tells us that the people you lead – once you get them *in the loop* – are the most powerful resource you have for accomplishing your goals and making your team, department, or entire organization more innovative.

We know getting people actively engaged is not an easy task. The challenge you face is complicated in part by the fact that the world of business has always been a bit schizophrenic. Few leaders would argue against the belief that people are, always have been, and always will be, their organization's most valuable asset. At the same time, it's not difficult to find organizations where those words ring hollow. They are spoken often when times are good and then choked back when times are not so good. This on-again, off-again scenario wears people out and ultimately threatens a company's long-term prospects no matter how rational the reason for explaining the split personality.

There are but a few short strides on the continuum between enthusiasm, skepticism, and cynical retreat, so it is critical that your leadership sends one consistent message about the value of people, no matter what else is happening.

Around the start of the year 2000, one of the main focal points of many companies around the world shifted dramatically. Almost overnight, a primary concern for many switched from being unable to hire enough good people to being able to terminate staff fast enough. Productivity numbers jumped, but so did evidence of employee burnout. There are times when job cuts are the only way for a company to right itself. But this kind of knee-jerk jump from "we've got to hire" to "oops, we've got to fire" sends a dangerous message – reinforcing the erroneous mechanical model instead of the more biological systems model of how organizations work. In this scenario, companies once part of the "Employees Are Our Most Important Asset" chorus became part of a nationwide downsizing trend. In the US alone, more than four million jobs were jettisoned in a two-year period early in this decade. That was despite research that shows companies that downsize significantly fare no better over the long term, and often do worse, than those that don't.

Life can be tough for the survivors in organizations going through difficult times. The situation is especially disheartening, however, in organizations that seem to value, respect and involve employees when things are going well, but lose sight of that priority when the economy tightens and immediately resort to the short-term solution of job cutting.

The result? Okay, Dilbert isn't real. He lives in a comic strip that satirizes the modern workplace. But creator Scott Adams was dead on when he penned a strip about this issue. The pointy-haired boss breaks the news to his staff that research shows employees are their company's ninth-most-valuable asset, not its first. Number eight? Carbon paper.

How much commitment, contribution, enthusiasm, and innovation should we expect from people who feel less valued than office supplies (and antique ones, at that)?

There are things you can do that will foster involvement and innovation, in good times and not so good, that won't necessarily put a strain on finances. For some, you really won't have to pay anything more than attention.

- *Ask for and act on people's ideas.* This is one of the most effective – and underused – ways to make people feel valued.
- *Sing up the unsung heroes.* In a June 2003 *Harvard Business Review* article, *Let's Hear It for the B Players*, authors Thomas J. DeLong and Vineeta Vijayaraghavan purport long-term performance – even survival – of companies depends on the commitment and contributions of their second-tier employees, not just the top players. This perception bucks the traditional wisdom that companies should focus foremost on their "stars." A little extra recognition will go a long way in making B players feel valued for their proven steadfastness.
- *Don't get swept up in the "Employees Are Our Most Important Asset" chorus.* Believe these words. Live them. The best strategy, however, may be never to say them. Let the melody stick in your head like one of those songs you just can't shake. Hum a little, maybe, but let your actions, rather than your words, demonstrate your unbending, ongoing conviction that people matter most.

Leading innovation can seem a daunting undertaking. But it's time to begin implementing your own version of LOOP Leadership. You can do this, and you will do it in the way only you can.

Where do you begin? Wherever you can and as soon as you can. No matter how long a trek it may seem lies ahead before you reach your innovation goals, just take a step. Get started.

Anne Lamott, author of *Bird by Bird: Some Instructions on Writing and Life*, passed on some advice that we find extremely applicable to the rocket science of leadership. Lamont writes about when her brother, as a ten-year-old, faced the daunting prospect of trying to write a report on birds – which he'd put off for three months – on the night before it was due.:

We were out at our family cabin . . . . and he was at the kitchen table close to tears, surrounded by binder paper and pencils and unopened books on birds, immobilized by the hugeness of the task ahead. Then my father sat down beside him, put his arm around my brother's shoulder, and said, "Bird by bird, buddy. Just take it bird by bird."

In the course of *Leading Innovation,* we hope we have persuaded you it's a costly oversight to underestimate and under use the potential of the people you lead. Doing so can be fatal and can perpetuate business practices that inhibit the aspirations and energy people bring to your workplace. They want to do good things. They want to work in ways that make a difference. Let them. Your success in leading innovation hinges on learning to unleash their talents, skills, gifts, and passions. Get them in the loop.

Index